Det Norske
Videnskaps-Akademi

II. Hist.-Filos. Klasse
Skrifter
Ny serie No. 17

On deadly violence
Kaare Svalastoga

Universitetsforlaget 1982
Oslo-Bergen-Tromsø

Fremlagt i fellesmøte den 11. september 1980

© Universitetsforlaget 1982
ISBN 82-00-06071-3
ISSN 0546-370X

Distribution offices:

NORWAY

P.O. Box 2977 Tøyen
Oslo 6. Norway

UNITED KINGDOM

Global Book Resources Ltd.
109 Great Russel Street
London WC1B 3NA

UNITED STATES and CANADA

Columbia University Press
136 South Broadway
Irvington-on-Hudson
New York 10533

Published with a grant from
The Norwegian Research Council
for Science and the Humanities

Printed in Norway by As Bryne Trykkeri

Contents

Preface

This investigation attempts to assess the state of theory and research on trends and causes of violent behavior.

The author has been helped by many social scientists and librarians both inside and outside Scandinavia. His deep indebtedness to them may be inferred from the text and the references. Financial contributions from the Danish Social Science Council has enabled him to collect information in libraries and research institutions in London and in Paris.

The Norwegian Research Council for Science and the Humanities has provided financial support for the printing of the treatise.

I am much honored by the decision of The Norwegian Academy of Science and Letters to publish the treatise in one of its series.

A special word of thanks goes to Grethe Hansen, Sociological Institute, University of Copenhagen, for careful and patient typing of several versions of the manuscript. Last but not least thanks to Kjell Herlofsen of The Norwegian Academy of Science and Letters for a successful fund-raising campaign.

Copenhagen, September 1982
Kaare Svalastoga

For Eiliv and Mette

1. Theory of Violence

... "the Earth is full of Violence". Genesis 6—13.

1.1 Varieties of Violence

Violent behavior is a common name for a large variety of behaviors all of which are more or less efficient attempts to threaten, hurt or kill a living organism.

the active part may be the environment, as in accidents, other organisms, as in homicide, revolution and repression, and war, or the organism itself, as in suicide.

Aromaa and Wolf (cf. Wolf 1972) developed a rank order of degrees of violence suffered by a victim. Since the scale was to be used in assessing violence endured, by means of interviews with victims, the more extreme degrees of violence were not included:

Aromaa-Wolf scale (1971—1972)
0) No violence experienced
1) Threats
2) Prevention of freedom of movement
3) Pushing
4) Hitting without visible marks
5) Hitting with visible marks
6) Wounds, no doctor
7) Wounds necessitating medical treatment

To this seven-step scale might be added

8) Violence producing a long period of hospitalization and (or) invalidity
9) Violence resulting in death

It is a highly plausible hypothesis that violence is more common the more modest its degree. Wolf (1976) analyzed survey data on violence experienced in Norway, Sweden, Denmark, and Finland, and found a general confirmation of this theory, although some deviations occurred, possibly due to sampling fluctuations. The distribution of the population on the violence scale is highly skewed, with 85% to 97% placed in the no-violence-experienced category.

A Danish survey institute presented results of a study undertaken in 1979 of the extent to which a sample of 1268 persons aged 18 years or more had been exposed to accidents, violence, theft, deceit or destructive behavior over a 12-month period (Thomle 1979).

The findings may be summarized as follows:

Exposed to	% mentioning
Road accidents	5
Other accidents	3
Violent behavior	4
Theft, deceit or destructive behavior	6
Total mentioning one or more of the above	15
N = 1268	

Males had been more exposed (20%) than females (11%).

Young persons had been more often exposed than older people. The urban population was likewise more exposed than the rural population.

From a study in Roxbury, Massachusetts, of a «fairly typical, lower-class, adolescent corner group, observed in its natural milieu» Miller et al. (1961) reported on aggressive behavior in the group. The report covered a group of 18 white Catholic boys aged 14—16 years.

Of 1490 aggressive acts altogether, 70% were addressed to other members of the group 12% to other local adolescents, 10% to adult social or recreation workers, 4% to school teachers and family members, and finally 4% to all others.

On the basis of 1395 aggressive acts analyzed in terms of intensity of aggression, the authors found that more than 9/10 of all aggressive acts were verbal, while at most 7% were physical attacks termed «simple» and here inferred to be unarmed.

Because of the difficulty of securing reliable information both in the present and in the past on all degrees of violence and in particular on the lower degrees of violence, the present study is limited to violence of the highest degree, that is violent death.

This highest level of violence also represents the greatest threat to the steady operation of social systems. But violence does not only appear as a threat to the operation of a social system. In competition for scarce resources the system's power of using superior violence may have survival value.

In fact for social systems of any size from the individual to the largest nation aggressive behavior is probably sufficiently often rewarding to ensure the prevalence of such behavior (cf. Bandura 1973).

Goode (1972) referred to force,[1] defined as threats of force and overt force, as one the four great universal social control systems, the other three being prestige, wealth, and affection.

Overt force can expropriate wealth, but cannot elicit respect or affection. Still every social system is seen as a force system because the social system contains mechanisms that reduce the frequency of overt force. All highly industralized societies are said to be high force systems by comparision with almost all societies that have gone before them. Modern industrial societies are less likely to be torn up by internal violent conflicts, and their governments are more likely to be backed by a consenting citizenry.

There are only five main types of violent death. Three types occur during the normal operation of a social system and will therefore collectively be referred to as operational violence: accidental death, suicide, and homicide. The fourth type of violent death occurs during challenges to the established hierarchical order of a social system and will here be collectively referred to as hierarchical violence. It includes all deaths due to internal imbalances of a social system.

The fifth type of violent death occurs when there is war, i.e. imbalance in the external relations of a social system. This includes all battle deaths and all civilian war deaths. Like hierarchical power in internal wars, it is territory that is scarce and desired in external war. The term territorial violence is therefore used to refer to external war.

Theories of violence will here be limited to theories that try to account for the occurrence of violence. Such theories attempt to describe conditions conducive to violence.

For a theory of violence to be general, it would have to account for all kinds of and degrees of violence from the mildest and most limited kinds of violence, e.g. threats expressed by one person or animal towards another person or animal, to the most most extreme and most comprehensive forms of violent behavior like human world wars. Actually existing theories of violence cover a considerable range of generality thus defined. There are theories like the frustration theory or the aggressive drive theory, which claim to be applicable to all kinds and degrees of violent behavior. But there are also theories that limit themselves to the explanation of one particular kind and one particular degree of violence. The preferred themes for the more specialized theories of violence have been suicide, revolution, and war. Such specialized theories will be discussed in later sections (5, 7, 8).

In the following theoretical review the factors or factor sets suggested by one or more authors as relevant to violence have been classified as follows:

Organism
Environment
Population
Technology
Rate of Change

It should be noted that this is the present author's classification, chosen because the five factor sets seem to refer to important determinants of violence regardless of type or degree, and also because they seemed to be suggested so often separately or in combination in the literature. Konrad Lorenz (1963) deserves the honor of having first pointed out this set of factors as important. The same set of factors reappeared in Tinbergen (1968), in van den Berghe (1974—1975), and in Montagu (1976).

1.2 Organism

Aristotle (384—322 B.C.) discussed the biological nature of man in the first book of his Politics. Man is said to be the best of the animals «when perfected» but the worst «when sundered from law and justice». Hence when devoid of virtue man is described as «the most unholy and savage of animals, and the worst in regard to sexual indulgence and gluttony».

McDougall (1917, 1908) considered pugnacity as one of man's ten inborn behavioral tendencies, which he termed instincts. He considered it likely that the instinct of pugnacity was stronger among modern Europeans than it was in primitive man. But he also noted a tendency to replace warfare by industrial and intellectual rivalry.

Simmel (1955, 1908) likewise considered «an a priori fighting instinct» the best explanation for a range of empirical observations tending to show that aggressive behavior is both common and easily provoked. He considered it well-known «that the mutual relation» of primitive groups was «almost always» one of hostility.

Freud (1917) presented an informal argument in support of the existence in man of both life, or sexual, drives and death, or aggression, drives (see in particular pp. 57—58 in Werke Bd. 13, London, 1947).

Aurdrey (1966) went further still, contending that man was subject to a territorial imperative which was «genetic and ineradicable».

Washburn (1966) stressed that throughout most of human history society has depended on young adult males to hunt, to fight, and to maintain the social order by violence. Individual role fulfillment could only be achieved «by extremely aggressive action, which was socially approved, learned in play, and personally gratifying». He furthermore pointed out that the basis for the majority of contemporary sports originally was preparation for war.

Corning & Corning (1972) likewise defended an evolutionary, adaptive theory of aggression. The basic circuitry for aggressive behavior is said to be wired at birth or very early in the developmental process. Biological variables giving different values by sex and age should therefore be able to account for at least part of the variability of violent behavior. It was considered significant that young males are responsible for most cases of human violence.

Storr (1972) stressed that homo sapiens ia a «violent and destructive species». We shall have to live with the fact of man's paranoid potential, cruelty, and destructiveness. Only in the very long run may we hope for modifications.

Scott (1975) stressed the aggressiveness of the primate male. In every primate species the males are, on the average, larger, stronger, and more aggressive than the females. The same basic situation of differential aggressiveness seems to exist in man, but it is complicated and modified by social training and by a large amount of individual hereditary variation. Scott presented a clear outline of his model of aggression:

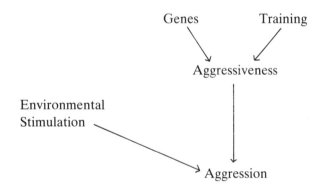

Scott belongs to the group of biologists who consider that man is a violence-prone animal: «evidence is consistent with the idea that apart from his cultural heritage man on the average shows a rather low threshold of aggression in both sexes» . . . (1975, p. 88).

Wilson (1975, pp. 254—255) considered aggression in man to be adaptive because it is «widespread» and «easily invoked». Aggressive responses in man are said to vary according to the situation «in a genetically programmed manner». It is the total pattern of responses that is adaptive and has been selected for in the course of evolution. Aggression may either be wholly innate or be acquired partly or wholly by learning. «The capacity to learn certain behaviors is . . . a genetically controlled and therefore evolved trait».

Murder is far more common in many vertebrate species than in man. The number of murderers per capita per time unit, with wars added in, is so relatively moderate in man that he must be considered one of the more pacific mammals (Wilson 1975, p. 247).

Ellis in a challenging paper (1977) argued strongly for a more biological orientation among sociologists. He suggested that human aggressive behavior could be explained in terms of the same causes that produce such behavior in non-human species, viz. genetic influences and biochemical influences. Ellis gave four references for evidence of genetic influences on aggressiveness in man: Vandenberg (1967), Maccoby & Jacklin (1974), Van den Berghe (1974), and Moyer (1975). Only Vandenberg and Maccoby & Jacklin produced detailed documentation.

Vandenberg (1967) analyzed comparisons of monozygotic twin differences and corresponding dizygotic differences. He contended that Holzinger's heritability index[2] provided an acceptable measure of trait inheritance. He concluded from values obtained that there was evidence of a strong hereditary component in sociability or extroversion — introversion. There was also evidence for a set of factors which he seems to equate to aggression. He suggested that «the manly virtues of aggressiveness and dominance may have been of evolutionary significance at one time, but perhaps forbearance and tolerance are at present more important for the survival of the human race».

Maccoby & Jacklin (1974) surveyed the literature on male and female aggressiveness and concluded «that males do appear to be the more aggressive sex, not just under a restricted set of conditions, but in a wide variety of settings» (p. 228). The authors listed altogether 94 studies, of which 54 showed higher male aggressiveness, 37 showed no difference between the sexes, and 5 showed higher female aggressiveness.

Females are less often the agents and also less often the objects of aggressive actions. Similar findings are said to exist for monkeys and apes.

The authors concluded that biological sex differences seemed to be involved in aggression for the following reasons:

1. Males are more aggressive than females in all human societies studied.
2. The sex differences in aggression appear early in life.
3. Similar sex differences in aggression are found among non-human primates.
4. Aggression is related to relative amount of male hormones (androgens).

In regard to biochemical influences Ellis referred to studies of testosterone level and aggression, to reports on biochemical treatment of psychosis, and to studies showing the influence of disease or malnutrition on indicators of aggression (Shah & Roth 1974, Weiss 1974). While the influence of biochemical medication on the behavior of psychotics seems well established (cf. Eisenberg 1973), the same cannot be said about the influence of testosterone level in the blood-plasma (cf. Persky et al. 1971, Kreutz & Rose 1972, Ehrenkranz et al. 1974).

The studies of the influence of disease and of malnutrition on indicators of aggression seem difficult to evaluate as to general importance. It may well be that disease more often is a protection against crime than a cause of crime; the same may hold for the relationship between malnutrition and aggression.

Ehrenkranz et al. (1974) stressed that the relationship between testosterone level and aggression is more controversial in man than among man's closest relatives, and that both positive correlations and absence of correlation have been reported.

It should be noted that Ehrenkranz and co-workers used a rather strong criterion for classifying a person as aggressive. They sampled a population of male prisoners aged 18—45 that had been subdivided into three categories by one of the researchers and the senior prison psychologist: Aggressive, Socially Dominant, and Non-aggressive. Twelve persons from each category were studied. The Aggressives were all in prison because of aggravated assault or murder, and most of them continued to show violent behavior in the prison. The socially Dominant were in prison for non-violent crimes, but they occupied high positions in inmate hierarchies. The Non-aggressives were also in prison for non-violent crimes; they did not play a conspicuous role in inmate groups. The aggressives had an average of 10 μg/ml testosterone in their blood-plasma, the socially dominant 8, and the non-aggressives 6. The difference between aggressives and non-aggressives and the difference between aggressives and all the others were statistically significant, as was also the difference between socially dominant and non-aggressives. In contrast self-reports on several psychological tests (57 variables) produced no significant correlation with testosterone level when the total group (N = 36) was considered.

There were no statistically significant differences in the height and weight of the prisoners in each of the three groups, and the range in mean age was less than 2 years (from 27.2 to 29.1 years).

In conclusion it must be accepted that in all behavior man is more or less influenced by biochemical and genetic forces. However, the documentation so far presented for a genetic factor in aggression still seems rather tentative, since it tends to be based on the comparison of categories of persons differing not only in genes but also in social environment experienced (males-females, uniovular twins — biovular twins).

Biochemical influences on aggressiveness may well be easier to establish particularly in psychiatry.

Asher (1978) reported briefly the results of research on aggressiveness carried out by the psychobiologist F. Goodwin, of the National Institute of Mental Health. His study of 26 men from the psychiatric ward of a military hospital documented that the most aggressive men tended to show higher levels of norepinephrine (a substance known to be associated with arousal and aggression) in the spinal fluid of the subjects. In contrast a heightened level of serotonin (a substance known from animal studies to aid in controlling impulsive behavior) was found among the least aggressive subjects.

Goodwin concluded that aggression and perhaps many other normally appearing behaviors involve a biological component. This biological component, according to Goodwin, was not necessarily genetically caused. It was always possible that a certain chemical production could be influenced by learning, malnutrition, and injury.

Baer (1978) expressed what he considered «the most basic, underlying concept of sociobiology and behavioral genetics» as follows:

$$P = G + E + (GxE)$$
where
G = value due to genotype
E = environmental deviation resulting from all non-genetic causes
GxE deviation resulting from genotype-environment interaction

A fairly extreme form of aggressiveness would be a tendency to continue any fight until victory or defeat with serious injury. Provided that the latter event is given a higher negative pay-off than the former event is valued positively (e.g. -20 against $+10$ for victory), then it can be shown that such a strategy has a negative pay-off and may be threatened by strategies with zero or positive pay-off. This so-called Hawk strategy is therefore not an evolutionary stable strategy (Smith 1978). A much more peaceful behavior would be to avoid fight by flight part of the time and only accept fight when meeting partners of similar strategy. But this so-called Dove strategy is not likely to be stable either, because it may be threatened by the superior pay-off to the Hawk-strategy in Dove encounters. Smith shows in fact that under the assumptions made in his example only a mixed strategy (playing Hawk somewhat more frequently than Dove, 8/13 against 5/13) is an evolutionary stable strategy which will not be threatened by mutations.

In another example Smith introduced an additional strategy: Bourgeois strategy. This strategy is a mixture of Hawk and Dove strategies according to the principle that the «owner» of the place will use Hawk strategy, the «not owner» will use Dove strategy.

The pure Bourgeois strategy is shown to be the only evolutionary stable strategy under the conditions postulated. The lesson taught by these game-theoretical examples seems to be a warning that species may risk extinction both from over-aggressiveness and from under-aggressiveness. Survival hinges upon the elaboration of a viable mixture of behavior: under certain conditions, a maximum of aggressiveness, under all other conditions less aggressive behavior.

Since the frustration-aggression theory originated in the biological tradition, it will be discussed here, although the theory may perhaps best be described as a mixture of a biological and a sociological explanation.

Freud (1953, 1920) seems to be the first scholar to introduce the concept frustration. The frustration of normal sexual desire is said to channel sexual behavior along deviant paths. One such deviant category comprises the sadists. Sadists are described as persons whose entire affectionate feeling is directed to causing their objects pain and torture (p. 315).

Dollard et al. (1939) developed these ideas further. They claimed that aggression is «always» a consequence of frustration. Frustration is said to have in addition other consequences, e.g. problem solving.

The authors do not enter much into the detailed mechanism involved in the frustration aggression sequence. They seem to imply that this sequence becomes invariant because the outcome is generally rewarding and hence subject to rapid learning.

Aggression stimulus strength is claimed to be directly dependent upon the amount of frustration, which again depends upon the number, degree, and repulsiveness of interferences with responses.

Frustration is seen as one of the conditions making for war. It is therefore concluded that wars become less likely if the intra-social level of frustration can be lowered. Criminality can be manipulated in the same way. In addition anticipated punishment will help.

Henry & Short (1954) considered that the relationship between suicide and the business cycle and the relationship between homicide and the business cycle (United States data c. 1900 — c. 1940) were consistent with a frustration-aggression theory. Both acts were interpreted by the authors as aggressive reactions to frustrations induced by economic macro-fluctuations.

A more modest and probably more viable theory of frustration was developed by Berkowitz (1962). Berkowitz asserted that frustration does not always produce aggression even in sublimated or displaced or internalized form.

As alternatives to aggression as a sequel to frustration he mentioned that it may be followed by withdrawal or by some kind of non-aggressive, constructive action.

A strong support of the frustration theory as applied to internal violent disturbances was expressed by editors Graham & Gurr (1969, pp. 621—644). As they reviewed the evidence on collective violence, they noted that «the assumption that men's frustration over social circumstances of their lives is a necessary precondition of group protest and collective violence», had received considerable support.

The adherents of the frustration-aggression thesis do not seem to have a sufficiently realistic set of assumptions. Frustration must be considered a common experience. Certainly more than 90 out of every 100 persons can report one frustrating event or more per year. In contrast, violent behavior is much more rare, partly because it has to compete with non-violent means, and partly because it has to compete with non-violent means, and partly because it meets with social rules that may either prohibit or seek to regulate violence. If 10% per year behave violently this is probably above maximum experience. We could then draw up the table shown below.

	Frustrated	Not frustrated	
Aggressive	a) 90	b) 10	100
Not aggressive	c) 810 900	d) 90 100	900 1000

Since the cells a and b are much more frequently known than the cells c and d, it is intelligible that theorists tend to generalize: most aggressives are frustrated. The table shows that so are most non-aggressives. Until more convincing documentation is available the frustration-aggression theory must be considered a not very plausible hypothesis.

1.3 Environment

Parsons (1947) stressed that all social behavior is ultimately the behavior of individuals. The aggressive dispositions of individuals are related to their hereditary constitution although the details do not seem to be understood. It is, however, likely that there will be wide variations in hereditary constitution in this as in other respects.

Parsons defined aggression as a disposition characterizing either an individual or a collectivity within a social system integrated in a moral order which defines reciprocal rights and duties. This disposition becomes an aggression when it includes an intention «illegitimately to injure» others. Such aggression is probably more often a sign of weakness and handicap than of biological strength.

«Whatever the hereditary potential, and whatever it may mean, there is an immense accumulation of evidence that in childhood aggressive patterns develop when security in some form, mostly in human relationships is threatened.»

One of the strongest arguments in favor of an explanation of violence in terms of the social environment comes from psychological learning theory. Bandura (1973) presented a thorough analysis of human aggression viewed as a consequence of differential social reinforcement of individual behavior.

«From the social learning perspective, human nature is characterized as a vast potentiality that can be fashioned by social influences into various forms» (Bandura p. 113, reprinted by permission).

To the extent, then, that man man appears violence-prone, it is not primarily the biological individual that is to blame, but rather the social system which has fashioned his behavior through differential rewards and punishments.

In modern everyday life a mixed pattern of reinforcement of aggression is considered typical. Aggression is sometimes rewarded and sometimes punished (p. 203).

With this strong emphasis on the social causation of aggression Bandura at the same time acknowledges that human behavior can only develop through the joint influence of sociological and biological influences. The capacity to learn is affected by genetic characteristics. Furthermore, a physically strong man will meet with more frequent rewards of violent behavior than will a physically weak person.

Selg (1975, 1971), who likewise approached aggression from the theory of learning, emphasized the very early age at which a child is able to learn aggressive behavior (18 months). Aggressive behavior patterns are learned in advance of all others and therefore more thoroughly learned. Selg also pointed to the strong reinforcement of aggressive behavior which makes it appear as privileged behavior (p. 177).

According to Nieburg (1963) some amount of violent behavior may be interpreted as conducive to the efficient operation of a social system be it a family, an association, a region, a nation or a group of nations.

All systems change. Individuals or groups can further or influence these changes if they are able to present credible threats of violence. This is not possible without some real violence. Law is said to «rest on» violence. Law creates stability. Where law is poorly represented, as in international relations, the threat of violence made credible by means of demonstrations of power tends to create stability and maintain peace.

Violence may function as an accelerator of the rate of change of a social system: «Suicides and crimes, however obscure and ambigious, threaten the world and thus change it».

Wolfgang (1958) launched the «subculture of violence» theory. Wolfgang maintained that the established facts in his study of homicide suggested that there might exist «a subculture of violence within the larger community culture that surrounds it», with sub-cultural conduct norms which may be at variance with those of the larger community. More specifically the subculture is described as an environment approving of «quick resort to physical aggression» under conditions not considered a valid excuse for aggression in the larger community. The subculture of violence theory as further outlined by Wolfgang (1966) rejects a biological explanation of aggression or violence and stresses that the chain of causation should be traced back to the «outside of the organism» although individual differences in reactivity are admitted. A more explicit statement of the subculture theory was given by Wolfgang & Ferracuti (1967). In this work the authors also gave information on the intellectual environment in which the subcultural theory grew up, with Albert Cohen's book on delinquent boys (1955) as a major inspiration.

The theory was given a succint interpretation in the 1967 formulation. It was maintained that its main tenets culd be listed in seven statements. Although several of these statements are concerned with definitions rather than propositions, there still are a few predictive assertions:

a. tendency to use violence applies to many situations in a violent subculture, making violence proneness a pervasive cultural theme.
b. the subcultural violence ethos is found in all age groups, but is most prominent in a limited age group «ranging from late adolescence to middle age».
c. the subculturals are violence-prone because they have learnt to be so.

Jackson Toby (1966) presented an interpretation of the «subculture of violence» theory. This subculture is found among segments of the population «unable to wield symbolic power». This probably means that they only with difficulty can argue their case either in speech or in writing. In such environments violence is a masculine ideal. This ideal is further nourished by deficient family structures which creates sex role uncertainty among young males.

An early representative of ideas similar to those of the subculture of violence school is the Finnish criminologist and statistician Veli Verkko. In his study of homicide and suicide in Finland he arrived at the conclusion that the whole of Finland was a subculture of violence and that an important cause was alcohol consumption. The latter variable was also pointed out as important by Wolfgang (1958).

Hackney (1969) established that the dichotomous variable South — Not South, where South means states belonging to the losing party in the American civil war, predicted state white homicide rate to the extent of explaining 29% of the total variance in the rate among 48 states. The total number of predictors including the South variable could explain 52% of the variation in rates. Holding constant 6 factors purporting to measure modernization, Hackney showed that there still was a partial correlation of + .49 between the South variable and state white homicide rate.

Gastil (1971) developed an index of Southernness giving a maximum score of 30 to the most purely Southern States[3] and a low score of 5 to the least southern ones.[4]

This index alone accounted for 75% of the variance in state homicide rates in 1960. Gastil stressed the importance of variations in regional cultures as conducive to variations in lethal violence, not necessarily, as the subculture theorists generally hold, because of different norms toward killing, but because their entire culture, including in the South a greater tendency to carry gun and knife, makes killing more likely.

The relative magnitudes of age-standardized murder rates are seen as determined by four additive and interactive conditions or states:

1. the universal condition of social life
2. the rates of certain other criminal activities
3. the extent and severity of «disorganized conditions»
4. the cultures or subcultures of the population (these vary in the extent to which the above conditions lead to lethal violence).

Loftin & Hill (1974) tried to improve the testing procedure used by Hackney and by Gastil. Loftin & Hill concluded that socio-economic variables were closely correlated with state homicide rates. They furthermore found the hypothesis tenable that the high levels of interpersonal violence in the South may be explained by the relative poverty of the South.

The subcultural theory was attacked by Ball-Rokeach (1973), who pointed out that the expected strong correlation between values and deeds failed to appear in the data analyzed by her (one sample survey and one study of prison inmates). However Magura (1975) questioned the validity of the rather abstract value-test used, as well as the validity of violence responses given by black, lower class, young males to white middle class female interviewers.

Steinmetz & Straus (1973) might be said to give theoretical support to the subcultural theory by emphasizing the hypothesis that intrafamily violence increases as one descends the social ladder. The theory that violence is learnt from the social environment through its re-enforcement of violent behavior must be considered the most plausible explanation of the relationship between individual violence and social environment. The subcultural theory may be seen as a special case of the more general learning-through-social-re-enforcement theory.

Thus the subcultural theory is limited to the part of violence defined as illegal by the greater society. It is natural to expect that such violence will be more frequent the weaker the bonds connecting a group or a subcultural area with the greater society, and the fewer alternatives to violence there are available. Although Erlanger (1974a, 1974b) was rather critical in his evaluation of the theory, it will here be assumed that its basic tenets will be confirmed.

1.4 Population

It should be observed that theorists both of preponderant biological persuasion and of dominant sociological persuasion have stressed the violence-aggravating influence of population growth, in particular when such growth occurs under conditions of limited resources.

Timasheff (1965) clearly held that certain wars were primarily caused by population pressure.

Tiger & Fox (1972) emphasized the fact that as long as man was a hunter, i.e. throughout 99% of his history, there was always ample space, always somewhere else to go. The motivation to kill and to conquer must have been weaker when it took so little to hand over one's own territory to uninvited visitors. With the introduction of the sedentary agrarian and later industrial civilization the control of violence became more difficult. We now live with «the dreadful truth that this very population pressure increases the incidence and extent of violence and multiplies its consequences so that it embraces women and children and the old and innocent. While congregation may not be a novel and root cause of violence, dispersion would certainly help in containing it» (p. 225).

Empirical studies of animal populations have frequently observed behavioral changes, including aggression, following increasing population pressure on scarce resources (Wilson 1975).

Calhoun (1962) showed that rats developed abnormal behavior of a potentially self-destructive kind in consequence of experimentally induced increase of density of rats per area. Females were unable to fulfill their normal maternal functions, and among males some became sexual deviants and cannibals and frenetically overactive, while others revealed pathological withdrawal tendencies.

Russel & Russel (1968) contended that violence in animal and human societies was a response to stress. This stress was seen as a function of imbalance in the relationship between a population and its resources. Violence can be seen as instrumental in re-establishing a tolerable balance between population and resources, but the instrument of violence is in the present age too destructive.

Myers et al. (1971) referred to a large amount of evidence affirming that crowding in laboratory and field populations of many mammals cause significant changes in behavior and physiology. The authors' work on rabbits confirmed this finding. Large loss in body weight and in the weight of metabolic organs, e.g. the spleen and the liver, were observed as a result of crowding. there was also impairment of the reproductive fucntion. Aggressive and sexual behavior increased with crowding.

It has been considerably more difficult to document the density-aggression theory on human populations.

Welch & Booth (1974) reported on an attempt to test the hypothesis with 65 nations as observational units.

The crowding variables were:

1. Persons per hectare
2. Dwelling units per hectare
3. Persons per dwelling unit

The dependent variables were:
1. Number of riots 1961—1963
2. The occurrence or non-occurrence of casualties as result of riots 1961—1963.

After entering industrialization and two other factors in the equation besides the crowding variables it was found that the crowding variables accounted for 14% of the total variance in incidence of disorder and for 19% of the variance in the casuality variable. Among the crowding variables the most important proved to be number of persons per dwelling unit.

McCarthy, Galle & Zimmern (1975) performed a test of the theory that density causes violence by studying the covariation of four density measures and two violence measures (homicide and aggravated assault) in 171 large (50,000 inhabitants or more in 1940) cities 1950 and 1970. In both years the best predictor among the density variables was precent of population at a density of 1.5 person per room or more, although its correlation with homicide declined from .7 in 1950 to .5 in 1970. A much better predictor was percent non-white:

$$r_{1950} = .85, r_{1970} = .82$$

The limited influence of the density variable was further stressed by the fact that density actually declined in these cities between 1950 and 1970, whereas homicide increased. It is also suggested that the goodness of the non-white percentage as homicide predictor may depend on a less efficient law-enforcement and hence less deterrence among non-whites.

Smith & Connolly (1977) studied the reaction of a group of preschool children to crowding and found some evidence that suggested increasing aggressive behavior above a level of density of four children per 100 square feet.

Carstairs (1969) expressed the view that human overcrowding tended to aggravate the stability threat presented by demoralized urban masses: «Unless the masses of our city poor can be persuaded that there is a future for them, too, in the Great Society, their morale is likely to crumble until vast human communities degenerate into the semblance of concentration camp inmates, if not even to that of Zuckerman's pathologically belligerent apes».

Other writers stressed the importance to violence avoidance of a population organization tending to minimize competition (Deutsch 1966, Zipf 1950), or of population homogeneity (Feirabend et al. 1969). Christie (1975, vol. 1, pp. 53—64, vol. 2, p. 270) maintained that two extreme types of social systems produce more violence than others:

1. The tightly knit social systems where the members are pulled together by durable ties, but still may react with love or hate towards each other.
2. The losely knit social systems where the members maintain no contacts or only superficial contacts with each other.

The tightly knit systems are violence-prone because there is no escape mechanism when social conflicts arise. The loosely knit systems are violence-prone because elementary rules of human decency lose their force in a system where members are strangers to each other.

Ehrlich & Ehrlich (1970 pp. 203—207) proposed tentatively that increasing population density is associated with increasing formality and elaborate etiquette as a mechanism for self-protection against the inevitable frictions of constant human encounters. The authors contrasted the formality of the densely living Japanese and Europeans with the more easy going style of the not so densely living Americans and Australians. The trend toward a more regulated, regimented, and formalistic life was interpreted as at least partly due to population growth.

Distance observed by partners in face to face interaction may be considered an appeasement manoeuvre. This could explain the smaller distance observed among acquaintances than among strangers (Cf. Heshka & Nelson 1972).

Biologist J. H. Crook (1978) looked on the manifestations of aggression in human society as «largely a cultural attribute». Aggression was so prevalent in modern society because this society was complex, overcrowded, overcompetitive, and overstratified.

1.5 Technology

Change in technology or in technology-related variables appear in many variants in theories of violence.

Some theories maintain that certain types of violence are connected with a certain stage of technology. Thus Boulding (1964, p. 77) noted that a strong case could be made for the proposition that wars represent a 5000 years interlude in human history (c. 3000 B.C. — c. 2000 A.D.). Boulding[5] asserted that the development of cities by «the expropriation through coercion of the food surplus from agriculture» took place during this interlude and produced wars. The pre-urban phase was not so warlike. The villages of this earlier period are more rarely walled in.

At the present time we are facedwith the problem of dispensing with wars. It is a «race between learning and disaster» (p. 91). The tools of destruction have increased so much in efficiency that the killing radius of major powers comprises the entire earth. Under such conditions either war must go or homo sapiens must go.

Criminologists have produced evidence suggesting a similar maladjustment between criminal violence and the industrial civilization producing a decline in criminal violence with increasing industrialization (Winslow 1970, Wolf 1968).

Winslow (1970) documented a correlation of $-.4$ between homicide and industrialization in about 30 nations in 1965. The same measure of industrialization also produced a correlation of $-.4$ with a measure of public disturbances.

Schilling (1968) stressed the importance of even modest technological advantages to conquest. He also contended that technological change had made national governments able to exercise greater command over their people and thereby contributed to the ability of governments to «wage more intensive and more sustained warfare». Increased efficiency in the techniques of mass destruction had increased the cost of wars both in terms of economic cost of destroyed material and in terms of lives lost (cf. also Bjöl (1970)).

A frequently met theory is an emphasis on technology as a factor that tends to act as a multiplier of the amount of violence. Thanks to his superior technology twentieth-century homo sapiens is not only able to be more constructive than his forebears but also to be more destructive, including higher self-destructive potential (cf. also sec. 1.2).

A deduction from this theory would be that populations with a high proportion of gun owners should, ceteris paribus, show more violence than populations with a low proportion of gun owners.

The proposition is not easily tested because of the many ways in which even closely related nations differ. The problem of firearms and violence was taken up by the National Commission on the Causes and Prevention of Violence in one of its staff reports. In this report Newton & Zimring (1969) estimated that Americans as of 1968 owned 90 million firearms, distributed on 24 million handguns, 35 million rifles, and 31 million shotguns. This estimate was based on data concerning American production of firearms 1899—1968 and imports 1918—1968, adding up to 102 millions, and in addition sample surveys 1966—1968 suggesting a maximum of 80 million firearms. Since the number of households as of 1968 was 60 millions, the commission estimate indicates an average ownership of 1.5 firearms per household. As of 1966 total accidents due to firearms constituted 15 per million for the United States, but for the Southern states the rate was 25 and the Eastern states had a rate of only 6, while the remaining states had a rate of 12 accidental deaths by firearm per million inhabitants.

At the same time the percentage of households owning firearms was 59 for the Southern states, 33 for the Eastern, and 49—51 for the remaining states. As the report says: «more gun accidents happen where more guns are» (ibid p. 29). It should be remembered that there is here as in many social situations a law of scale: the persons only hurt far exceed in number the persons killed. The report suggests a 7:1 ratio in this case both for accidental and non-accidental injuries and deaths (p. 29 note 2).

In addition the authors show that Detroit during the 1960s experienced a growth in the number of hand-gun permits issued, and that this was correlated with a rising level of accidental deaths from firearms. They also presented urban data documenting a consistently higher use of firearms in homicide, robbery, and aggravated assault in 1967 in cities situated in high gun-ownership regions as against cities in low gun-ownership regions. They concluded that gun use in violence rises and falls with gun ownership (cf. also Seitz, 1972).

Hawkins & Ward (1970) compared different regions in Australia, where some regions follow the British model (police force normally unarmed) and some follow the American model (police force normally armed). There was less violence in English mode regions, but the results must be considered inconclusive, since no attempt was made to take into account differences in violence-provoking stimuli other than the one to be tested between the two types of regions.

In reference to mortality risk from firearms attacks as against attacks with knives, the two dominant tools used in homicide in the United States, Newton and Zimring pointed out that the firearms were about five times as lethal as were knives and firearms were used in 63% of all homicides in the USA in 1967 as against 25% killed by knives.

The authors tried to estimate ownership of handguns per 100,000 population and gave the following figures for Finland, Great Britain, and the USA:

Finland under 500
Great Britain under 500
USA 13,500

Comparable figures for Austria are 3000 and this was the highest figure for a European nation, although only Great Britain was included among the larger.

Zimring (1968) concluded a review of the problem of gun-control effect by the following guarded proposition:

«The only unlikely conclusion is that weapon dangerousness does not affect the gross expectable homicide rate».

Zimring arrived at this conclusion because of the following facts:

1. The majority of victims of homicide are relatives, friends, and acquaintances.
2. Most homicides resulted from altercations.
3. Victims of homicide are distributed by race and sex as victims of non-fatal attacks (serious assaults).
4. Only 30% of the victims of fatal gunshot attacks in 1967 in Chicago were wounded by more than one shot.
5. In at least 54% of the situations leading to homicide the offender or the victim or both had been drinking.
6. He also noted that the Chicago 1966 distribution according to type of homicide instrument was approximately the following per 10 homicides:
Firearms   5
Knives   3
Other weapons   1
No weapons   1
7. He reported the dangerousness of or risk of death from use of firearms as five times that of knives on the basis of a table from Chicago 1965—1967 covering attacks known to the police.

Murray (1975) stressed the multiple social determination of violence and documented *inter alia,* that American states with a high percentage of blacks were more likely to have both many homicides and many firearm accidents assaults, and robberies. Another important correlate was percent interstate migrants. Murray found little or no improvement in regressional prediction by including data on the severity of gun-control laws in addition to the set of social predictors. There might of course still have been a significant improvement in prediction if variables measuring actual handgun ownership rather than rules of ownership had been used.

1.6 Rate of Change

Malthus (1959, 1798) presented the first and most dramatic theory on differential rates of growth and its consequences. The variables compared were population and means of subsistence. Population was assumed to grow at a constant *rate* which could produce doubling every 25th year or an annual rate of growth of .0281 given a favorable environment. The means of subsistence were assumed to be capable of growth by a constant *amount* each year, thereby steadily increasing, but much more slowly than population. A possible annual growth series for both variables was given by the author and may be rendered thus:

Time (t)	0	25	50	
Population (P)	1	2	4	or $P_t = (1.0281)^t$
Means of subsistence (S)	1	2	3	or $S_t = 1 + .04\,t$

As no population can survive when the means of subsistence fail to provide life maintenance, it follows necessarily that either fertility or mortality or both must be changed so as to reduce the pressue of population on its resources. Although Malthus mentioned various methods, e.g. delayed marriage for fertility reduction, he seems to have considered that the normal method of adjusting to scarce resources was by way of increasing mortality through what he termed misery and vice (see in particular p. 49). Misery clearly referred to such extremes of poverty, malnutrition, and such severe diseases as would cause an increase in the annual death toll. Vice seems to have been used to refer to types of morally rejected sex behavior that might reduce fertility (p. 34) but also to war activity, which was specifically mentioned, and perhaps by implication to all kinds of violent death.

When Darwin (1929, 1858) coined the concept struggle for existence, he specifically referred to Malthus' population theory «applied with manifold force to the whole animal and vegetable kingdoms».

A struggle for existence was seen as an inevitable consequence of the high rate of growth characterizing all organic beings if unchecked. Otherwise, because growth tended to be geometric, any species would fill up the world in due time. Hence, as more individuals are produced than can possibly survive,

26

there must in every case be a struggle for existence, either one individual with another of the same species, or with the individuals of distinct species, or with the physical conditions of life (p. 48).

Darwin does not seem to mention the rate of growth of means of subsistence, probably because the only reasonable general assumption would be zero growth when all animals and plants and not only homo sapiens are considered.

In Marx's famous preface to the monograph *Zur Kritik der politischen Økonomie* (1859), the «productive forces» *(Produktivkräfte)* appear as eminently changeable while the socio-economic system and the cultural system lag behind, with revolutionary events as a consequence.

Ogburn (1922) made the observation that «the various parts of modern culture are not changing at the same rate, some parts are changing much more rapidly than others» . . . Since the parts of culture are interdependent, a rapid change in one part of culture requires readjustments through other changes in the various correlated parts of culture. The numerically most important type of leadlag relationship was one where some part of the material culture was changing whereas the adaptive culture only changed more slowly or only changed later. Because the material culture and its adaptive culture, e.g. industry and education, are interdependent, a period of maladaption or maladjustment sets in until the lag has been abolished.

Thus the adjustment of American society to the early industrial environment was in the early period of industrialism characterized by much maladjustment in the form of human suffering. Only after a time-lag of about 45 years did American society establish workmen's accident compensation laws.

Hawley (1978) stressed the difference between the exponents of increase in scale and complexity. Populations and their activities do not increase as fast as their number of relations. In consequence rapid population growth tends to generate a steep rise in the cost of moving people, goods, and messages.

Several authors have explained violence as the outcome of imbalanced growth processes, a model also suggested in Boulding's analysis. Thus Tinbergen (1968) explained man's present violent behavior as the consequence of the severe imbalance created by the very rapid cultural evolution and the much slower biological evolution.

Wars, in particular, have been explained as consequences of differential rates of growth (Kuznets 1954, Boulding 1966, Björl 1970, Svalastoga 1976, 1978).

Andreski (1964, p. 119) wrote:[5] «A situation becomes very propitious for empire building when one nation suddenly develops, or acquires in some way, weapons or tactics or forms of military organization which are better than those of the surrounding peoples». The Romans conquered because of superiority in organization and tactics. The modern Europeans were able to acquire colonies chiefly because of superiority in arms . . .» a victory in a future war can only be the fruit of superior technical inventiveness, and could never result from the mere multiplication of the armaments existing at present» (ibid. p. 140).

Galtung (1964) defined his concern as aggression in the sense of a drive to hurt and harm, which was seen as «pervasive, important, and catastrophic with modern technology as a multiplier». Aggression was considered most likely to arise in elements in a social system that occupy different ranks on a set of socially significant ranking factors. Among the TT, UT, TU, and UU, the UT and TU are more likely to kill.[6] In the course of his paper the author outlined a recipe for revolutions where the dependence of disequilibration on differential rates of change appears clearly: expand the population of academic graduates, contract or leave unchanged the number of academic jobs, expand mass education, leave unchanged the (low) standard of living and the (near zero) political influence.

Brzezinsky (1976) maintained that during he nineteenth century the conditions of life changed faster than the way of thinking, whereas during the twentieth century the thought-ways changed faster than the way of living. He considered that the diffusion of reading ability had led to an activiation and politicization of the hitherto hard-to-move masses. This leads to demands and overtaxing of the political system.

Norman (1962, p. 9 and p. 48) pointed to the differential rates of change of vehicle (from horse to motorcar) as against road (roads built for horsetraffic to roads *mostly* built for horsetraffic) as a partial explanation of motorcar accidents. For a similar emphasis see Svalastoga (1970).

1.7 Towards a Consensus Theory

There seems to have developed a certain amount of consensus among some of the major contributions toward the theory of violent human behavior in general. this consensus is most easily seen if one analyzes the list of explanatory variable used. It is true that dissensus also appears but mainly in regard to the weight that should be given to human biology in the explanation of violent behavior.

A syndrome of five factors or sets of factors carries the main explanatory burden in most comprehensive theories of violence proposed since 1963. The five factors were all mentioned that year in Lorenz's *Das sogenannte Böse*, Vienna 1963.

They reappeared in Tinbergen's 1968 paper. They appeared again in van den Berghes violence theory (1974—75) and also in Montagu (1976).

These five factors are as already mentioned:

1. Organism
2. Environment
3. Population
4. Technology
5. Rate of Change

A minimnum content of this consensus theory might read as follows:

The individual human being is equipped genetically with a potential for aggression which is variable and which may be and customarily is socially re-enforced. The exact interrelationship between biological and sociological factors in aggression remains to be known.

This normal individual tendency towards the use of violence was not problematic in the past history of mankind, when population concentrations in this world were few and far between, when the technology of warfare was only modestly destructive, and where social change proceeded at a very slow pace, leaving ample time for the developments of viable customs.

But the modern world with its population explosion, its technological revolutions at shorter and shorter intervals, and with its, in consequence, highly stepped-up rate of social change and frequent experience of the maladjustments of differential rates of change is a much more dangerous environment. In this environment an aggressiveness that had survival values at earlier stages of development may possibly be self-destructive.

The only valid cure for this dilemma and for increasing similar problems in the future is a cure based on science rather than magic.

Lorenz (1973, 1963) maintained that aggression was a dominant drive among animals. The great majority of vertebrate species are said to attack members of their own kind. Aggressiveness is also functional in securing more efficient utilization of the resources of an area, in protecting the young, and in giving the next generation optimal parents in regard to survival. Man suffers from an excessive aggression drive. His intelligence has produced a culture that influences him (see p. 318 last five lines).

Culture developed so fast that human instincts could not keep pace with it. This stepped-up rate of change is one of the main sources of evil in human society.

The discovery of artificial weapons opened up new ways of killing and destroyed the balance between aggression-reducing mechanisms, which are weak in man, and the capacity to kill members of the same species. The increase in the number of people belonging to a society is another aggression-promoting factor.

Tinbergen (1968) likewise seems to place the major stress on biological factors and evolution. Man is said to be akin to many other animals in fighting his own species. But it is added that the human species is the only one in which fighting is disruptive and that man is the only mass-murdering animal. It is considered likely that man still carries with him the animal heritages of group territoriality.

At the same time Tinbergen stressed that man's aggressive tendencies are highly variable rather than constant and depend on both external and internal influences. Tinbergen also stressed the importance of the traditional biological emphasis on «survival value and evolution». The main explanation for man's present maladaptation is to be found in the differential rates of change whereby cultural evolution has come to outpace biological evolution:

«There are good grounds for the conclusion that man's limited behavioral adjustability has been outpaced by the culturally determined changes in his social environment, and that this is why man is now a misfit in his own society».

Cultural evolution has caused the population explosion, the industrial civilization with its pollution, efficient communication permitting continous provocation of aggressive tendencies, a concept of martial honor tending to make wars more destructive, and efficient destructive tools that will kill enemies at a distance out of reach of the victim's appeasement, reassurance and distress signals.

Van den Berghe (1974, 1975a) outlined a theory of human aggression which tries to explain aggression, territoriality, and hierarchy among men.

The general cause of these three phenomena is resource competition, which again comes about through the pressure exerted by an increasing population on not so rapidly increasing resources.

Resource competition becomes more severe with increasing technology because this technology produced unlimited social needs in contrast to the relatively quickly sated basic biological needs.

It is contended that aggression, territoriality, and hierarchy among men are at least in part biogenically determined.

Such partial determination seems to be the best explanation for the similarity of «the basic species-wide aspects» of aggression, hierarchy, and territoriality.

Van den Berghe thus rejects both extreme instinctivism and extreme environmentalism. As the present author reads him, he stresses in particular the biological aspects of human behavior, but does not seem to think that biological factors will explain the major part of the variability in aggression, although they will explain a significant part.

Because of severe resource competetion, men have become more aggressive than most mammals.

Territoriality was defined as a tendency to fight for and to defend a certain space or territory. Hierarchy was defined as the tendency to fight for and to defend positions of privilege in a social system.

In his monograph (1975b) Berghe insisted more strongly than before on the theory that man is the most violent animal «the most sweepingly destructive on the planet» (p. 44).

Montagu (1976) developed a theory of violence where there is room for «some genetic contribution», but where learning is more important because «we truly become . . . whatever, within our genetic limitations we learn to be».[7] There is a genetic potential for aggression but only when environment rewards aggression, will it also appear in behavior. It can be inferred from our past over the last five million years that cooperation and mutual aid have been more dominant than competition and mutual hostility.

Montagu furthermore considered that the cultures of the gatherer-hunter peoples were non-aggressive but that the huge increase in population over the recent past had produced more violence. On the whole the rate of change during the recent past was considered to have «greaty» accelerated and «immensely» increased the problems with which mankind is confronted. Technology is an important factor, because societies usually became more violent and vastly more efficient in their destructiveness with the growth in their technology.

2. Demography of Violent Death

2.1 On Richardson

Among contributors to research on violence one of the greatest is Lewis Fry Richardson 1881—1953, British phycisist, meteorologist, and social scientist of Quaker tradition. The impact of his work on violence will be noted in the present work as well as in many other contributions.

One of his many strokes of genius was his delimitation of the research area.

Richardson limited his study to violence by men producing deaths in other men. Secondly he included all types of such violent death, not wars only, nor revolutions only, nor homicides only. Thirdly he related the violent deaths to the total number of deaths in the population for the same period of time.

The advantages obtained by leaving aside violence not causing deaths are several.

Violence as conventionally defined ranges from threatening to killing. However, threats are much more rarely counted than are murders. Statistics on deaths are on the whole also likely to be the most reliable data on violence. Richardson's procedure enables the researcher to concentrate his energy on the most important, most available, and most reliable data.

By including several types of fatal violence he was able to compare the relative importance of the various types. By relating deaths by violence to all deaths he also showed how the importance of violent deaths for given time and space could be compared to medical statistics on the relative importance of causes of death.

Of every 1000 persons born 1000 persons die. If they died in the time interval 1820—1945 (both end-years included) 16 of them would die in war, in revolution, or from homicide, according to Richardson's estimate (1960, p. 153). Richardson summed the numbers of deaths in all «deadly quarrels» having more than 3162 deaths. This gave 46.8 million people for the indicated range of years (126). Next he estimated the number of persons killed in common homicidal situations for the same range of years (pp. 144—146).

He did this by first estimating a world murder rate per year and per million population. He observed that several large nations showed a relatively modest range in murder rate per million persons, e.g. USA 1932:85, 1936:62, Russians in Russia 1908—1912:40, British India 1914—1918:30. A weighted average of these three national samples gave 32 murders per year per million. The weights used were the population size at or about 1874—75, the middle of the interval 1820—1945. He estimated a world population at that midpoint time by extrapolation from data given by Carr-Saunders and found it to be 1358 millions.

Let x be total number of murders 1820—1945, then we estimate

$$x_{est} = 1358 \times 32 \times 126 = 5.475 \times 10^6.$$

Richardson rounds off upward to 6×10^6 (p. 125). He contends, however, that this number only counts murder cases and not the total number of persons killed in murder cases[1] (see pp. 144—146). On the basis of figures for England and Wales 1935 and 1936 he concluded that an estimate of the world total of persons murdered was

$$6 \times 10^6 \times \frac{303}{186} = 9.774 \times 10^6$$

which is rounded off to 9.7×10^6, distributed with 3.0 million with one victim, 4.6 million with 2 victims, and 2.1 million with 3 victims (p. 146). He then plots $\mu = \log_{10}$ (number killed in quarrels) on the X axis against $\phi = \log_{10}$ (number of quarrels per unit range of dead). See Fig. 4, p. 149.

By interpolation he estimated that altogether 2.9 million people had died in deadly quarrels in which from 4 to 3162 persons died over the 126 years.

The total number estimated to be killed in deadly quarrels 1820—1945 was therefore $46.8 + 2.9 + 9.7 = 59 \times 10^6$ persons. If a mean annual death rate of 20 per thousand is assumed to take its toll of a mean world populaton of 1.5×10^9 population over 126 years, we obtain 3.8×10^9 persons. We conclude that the proportion of persons who died in deadly quarrels is $\frac{16}{1000}$ or 1.6% among all deaths.

According to Richardson's counts and estimates, deadly quarrels with numerous quarrel deaths are few in number, whereas deadly quarrels with only one or a few quarrel deaths are much more frequent (cf. Table 2.1). Thus Richardson found only 94 conflicts in the world during the period 1820—1945 of such seriousness that $10^{3.5}$ persons or more were killed, but the total number killed in these 94 conflicts amounted to 47 million persons.

In contrast he estimated that there were about 400,000 conflicts of more moderate seriousness where the number of persons killed ranged from $10^{.5}$ to $10^{3.5}$. But the total number killed in these conflicts was estimated to be only about 3 million persons. As a consequence the total number killed in conflicts of severity $10^{.5}$ killed or more is only decreased by 6% if the approx. 400 000 conflicts in the range $10^{.5} - 10^{3.5}$ are left out.

Richardson thus presented the best available evidence for the generalization: most fatal conflicts are small conflicts (few deaths), large catastrophies are rare.

Table 2.1 Richardson's estimates

Log_{10} (quarrel deaths)	Number of quarrels	Total number of deaths (10^6)	
$7 \pm 1/2$	2	36	
$6 \pm 1/2$	5	6.7	
$5 \pm 1/2$	24	3.4	
$4 \pm 1/2$	63	.75	
Total by count			46.8
$3 \pm 1/2$	354	.30	
$2 \pm 1/2$	5630	.40	
$1 \pm 1/2$	397000	2.2	
Total by interpolation			2.9
$0 \pm 1/2$	6000000	9.7	
Total by estimation			9.7
Grand total number of estimated deaths in fatal quarrels in the world 1820—1945			59

2.2 On Death

The present study follows in Richardson's footsteps, because violence research is limited to types of violence resulting in deaths, because a comprehensive search for such violence is undertaken, and because deaths by violence are related to all deaths for given time and space.

The present investigator departed from Richardson on two points only:

1. It was considered desirable to include deaths by self-violence and deaths by accident, because both these categories are commonly referred to as death by violence and also because these additional violence categories are important causes of death. The deaths by suicide and the deaths by accident must furthermore be assumed to be primarily socially caused.

2. The present assessment of the demographic importance of violent death will be more limited in time and particularly in space than Richardson's

investigation. It will be limited to the 60 years 1900—1959 or 1901—1960 and will only deal with four nations: The United Kingdom, France, Germany, and Russia (USSR).

Homo sapiens is subject to the risk of violent death not only from birth to death but also from conception to birth. The intrauterine career of man is in general a biological task rather than a sociological task and will not be studied here.

When foetal death is caused by human interference it is eo ipso a social datum. However, not all social data are equally accessible to sociological research. Abortions are in general only reliably observable when they are defined as legal, so broadly defined as legal that illegal abortions become negligible. This has not normally been the case in Western civilization. The increasing tolerance of induced abortion is a recent development.

Violent death is here defined as comprising five causes of death, distributed among three categories of violence:

1. Operational violence
   1.1 Accident
   1.2 Suicide
   1.3 Homicide
2. Hierarchical violence (collective violence, revolution, repression)
3. Territorial violence
   a) Military war deaths
   b) Civilian war deaths

The non-violent deaths, i.e. all deaths except those covered by the above list, are conventionally ascribed to non-social causes. Of course closer investigation might well establish that numerous non-violent deaths might depend at least in part on the social environment.

In particular, an increasing standard of living among the total population or among its lower (less privileged) strata might well further increase life expectation and reduce the death rate from so-called non-violent causes.

While there seems to be general agreement that mortality in general has a social component even among the causes of death defined in biological terms, there may be considerable uncertainty as to the age of this relationship as well as it strength.

Pressat (1973) expressed the opinion that the death rate was unrelated to social status up to a fairly recent time because of the inefficiency of medicine and frequent and virulent epidemics. But at least from the sixteenth century it is known through Hollingsworth's study on the British nobility and Henry's study on The Genevan bourgeoisie that the upper strata had an advantage of 5—10 years over the rest of the population, who could not expect to live more than 25 years on the average.

The relative contribution to the death toll by social inequality expressing itself in reduced life expectation can conveniently be analyzed if the following assumptions are made:

	Relative size	Life expectation	Death rate per year
Upper class	α	kx	$\dfrac{1}{kx}$
Lower class	$1-\alpha$	x	$\dfrac{1}{x}$
Total system	1	$\alpha kx + (1-\alpha)x$	$\dfrac{1}{\alpha kx + (1-\alpha)x}$

$$0 < \alpha \leq \frac{1}{2}$$

$k > 1$ Total population $= N$

Surplus deaths each year in lower class

$$N(1-\alpha)\left(\frac{1}{x} - \frac{1}{kx}\right)$$

Relative contribution of surplus deaths to total annual deaths is given by equation (1) below which may be simplified and give equation (2).

$$(1)\ Y = \frac{\text{Surplus death per year in lower class}}{\text{Total deaths each year}}$$

$$= \frac{N(1-\alpha)\dfrac{1}{x} - \dfrac{1}{kx}}{N\left(\dfrac{1}{\alpha kx + (1-\alpha)x}\right)}$$

$$(2)\ Y = (1-\alpha)\,\alpha(k-1) + (1-\alpha)^2\left(1 - \frac{1}{k}\right)$$

It will be seen that y increases with the value of k, the multiplier indicating the factor to multiply lower class life expectation with to obtain upper class life expectation. For constant value of k the handicap of the lower class increases with the decrease of the relative size of the upper class, or other-

36

wise expressed: the lower class handicap as measured by y becomes larger the larger the size of the lower class. From equation (2) it will be seen that an upper class advantage corresponding to $k = 2$ gives for

$$\alpha = .05 \; y = \frac{399}{800} \doteq \frac{1}{2} \; \text{and for} \; \alpha = .5 \; y = \frac{3}{8}$$

The above equation may be used to assess the proportion of surplus deaths in the lower class when, as in sixteenth-century England and Geneva, the advantage of the upper class is taken to be

$$k = \frac{7.5 + 25.0}{25.0} = 1.3 \; (\text{cf. Pressat 1973})[2]$$

and α — the size of the upper class is taken to be .01.

We obtain annual excess mortality of the lower 99% of the population as a proportion of total annual (cf. equation (1) after multiplying out the x's only) mortality:

$$\frac{\dfrac{.99 \cdot \dfrac{.3}{1.3}}{1}}{(.01 \times 1.3) + .99} \doteq .23$$

or 23% of total annual mortality.

When social inequality is associated with a surplus death toll, it does not follow that a given society will experience the theoretically computed reduction of its death toll by introducing greater equality. The consequences would depend on many unknown factors such as, for example, the efficiency of the transfer of resources from the upper class to the lower class.

The difference in life expectation between the sexes was, in pre-industrial Europe, about two years in the favor of the female sex, according to Pressat (1973). Pressat attributed the difference to biological causes because of its regularity and because it was associated with a strong (25—30%) surplus infant mortality of the male sex.

The increasing life expectation difference between males and females with increasing industrialization and urbanization has caused an approximate quadrupling in the life expectation difference from about 2 years to about 8 years. According to the Danish Statistical Yearbook 1978, the difference in France was 7.6 years in female favor in 1973 and 3.4 years around 1900.

Comparable increases from about 1900 to about 1975 were for England

and Wales from 3.9 to 6.4 years, for Germany from 3.4 to 7.6 years, for USA from 2.4 to 7.7 years, and for Sweden from 2.5 to 5.8 years.

Pressat interpreted this increase as mainly caused by the following four factors, of which three are much more common among males and one much more common among females.

1. Accidents
2. Alcoholism
3. Smoking
4. Hygienic standard (female advantage)

The most promising road towards reduction of socially caused inequalities in mortality may well be, as envisaged by Pressat (1973), a lifting of the general hygienic standard and improved protection of the population from malignant environments.

In France 1966—1970 the rate of infant mortality by social class ranged from 12 per thousand among «professions libérales et cadres supérieurs» to 30 per thousand among unskilled workers (manoeuvres), 1970.

Bouthoul (1970) pointed out that mankind had created certain destructive institutions apart from war. He listed the following five:

1. Infanticide
2. Maltreatment of young people
3. Monasticism
4. Slavery
5. Repressive law

These institutions might function as direct killers (Infanticide) or they might reduce a person's life expectation by making his life more miserable or more risky, or they tended to reduce the chance of producing offspring (Monasticism).

While Bouthoul thus stressed the many-faceted destructive capacity of the social system, Menninger (1966, 1938) pointed to the many ways in which a person could behave so as to further his own destruction apart from direct suicide. He listed ascetism and martyrdom, alcohol addiction, criminality and behavioral disorders.

It is also possible to interpret all these self-destructive mechanisms as responses to a social system that has failed to develop adequate techniques for socializing its weakest members (cf. also Baechler 1970, p. 60).

2.3 Violent Deaths in Four European Nations 1900—1960

The intention of this section is to assess the demographic importance of violent death for a limited number of years 1900—1959 or 1901—1960 and for a limited number of the larger and politically more important European nations: The United Kingdom, France, Germany, and USSR (Russia).

Data or estimates on all types of violent deaths in these nations during the designated 6/10 of a century were related to the total number of deaths from all causes, so as to assess for given time and place the demographic impact of a certain violent cause of death.

The central part of this section consists of four sets of figures, one for each of the nations mentioned and each set presenting actually recorded figures or estimated figures (est.) for each of five causes of death (See Table 2.2).

Data are presented for the United Kingdom 1901—1960. The United Kingdom was defined as England and Wales, Scotland, and Ireland 1901—1920, and as England and Wales, Scotland, and Northern Ireland 1921—1960. It will be seen that the two largest violent killers are war (3.4% of all deaths) and accidents (3.1% of all deaths). Suicide came next with a little less than 1%. In contrast, the two other causes of violent death proved to be of modest numerical importance: homicide 5 per 10,000 deaths, and hierarchical violence, 3 per 100,000. Hierarchical violence may be under-represented, in which case it is likely that the homicide figures are slightly exaggerated.

Altogheter 7% died violently in the United Kingdom among all who died in the interval 1901—1960.

Hollingsworth (1957) reported the percentage of all male deaths at age 15 and upwards in British ducal families which were due to violence. From his description it may be seen that deaths due to war and internal disorders were included. Accidental deaths may not be included nor deaths by suicide and homicide. Hollingsworth's figures were adjusted by the present author to give the percentage of all male deaths by taking into account Hollingsworth's survivors' table (Table 10). The percentage of all male deaths due to violence as defined by Hollingsworth then becomes:

	%violent deaths
1330—1479	28
1480—1679	11
1680—1729	7
1730—1779	3
1780—1829	4
1830—1879	7

According to Hollingsworth, the 1330—1479 category is more hypothetical than the others.

Hollingsworth (1964—65) documented that the male part of the British nobility (peerage) born 1875—1899, a total of 1059, could be classified as follows:

		% N = 1059	% N = 765
Still living	294		
Died non-violently	570		
Died violently	195	18.41	25.49
	1059		

These were the generations that carried the burden of the first World War. The abnormally high figure of 25% of all deaths so far due to violent causes is most closely comparable in time with the figure presented here. it suggests that war in particular samples its victims more intensively from the higher social strata.

Table 2.2 also presents comparable data on France 1900—1959. Again war (5.3% of all deaths) and accidents (3.2% of all deaths) are the largest violent killers, with suicide in third place (1.1% of all deaths). As for the United Kingdom, homicide and hierarchical violence are numerically unimportant (respectively 10 per 10,000 deaths, and 2 per 10,000 deaths).

Germany 1900—1959 reveals in some respects the same general distribution as the United Kingdom and France but in some respects it is different. Again war and accidents are the large killers, but in Germany war was about five times as important as a cause of death as accidents. Next in importance again comes suicide, while homicide and hierarchical violence are more rare. However, hierarchical violence is 30 times as common as in France, chiefly due to the Hitler Period (1933—1945). Germany is a collective name for Imperial Germany, the German Republic, and West Germany. Altogether 19.1% of all deaths were violent.

While the three nations hitherto discussed differed considerably in the degree to which deaths were caused by wars, they revealed a striking similarity in the incidence of the violent deaths that occur during the normal operation of society. The sum of accident + suicide + homicide gives 38 for the United Kingdom Kingdom, 44 for France, and 44 for Germany. In other words Western Europe c. 1900—c. 1960 was at least in its leading parts a social system operating with a minimum demographic cost of 4% of all deaths per year.

For Russia (USSR) no figures on operational violence were available. The estimates given are the French relative frequencies. The estimate for accidents may be too low (cf. below sec. 4). The demographic career of Russia (USSR) is strikingly different from that of Western Europe because of the impact of the Russian revolution in 1917 and its aftermath, which, according to the sources used, makes hierarchical violence the second largest killer in Russia (USSR) in this period. The total number killed by war is also very high, as in Germany, but its relative importance is smaller in Russia (USSR) than in Germany.

The annual average number of deaths in the 60-year period studies is

$$\bar{D}_t = \frac{1}{60} D_t$$

where
D = deaths
t = total
The annual average death rate per capita may be written

$$\bar{D} \bar{P}^{-1}$$

Hence the inverse is

$$\bar{D}^{-1} \bar{P} \qquad \text{and}$$

$$\bar{D} (\bar{D}^{-1}\bar{P}) = \bar{P}$$

Let $\bar{V}$ = average number of violent deaths of some kind per year then

$$\bar{V} \bar{P}^{-1} = \bar{V} \bar{D}^{-1} \times \bar{D} \bar{P}^{-1}$$

It follows that the relative figures given in Table 2.2 should be divided by 10^3 and then multiplied by the mean death rate to give rate per unit of the mean population. Thus assume that mean mortality of the period is 15×10^{-3} for the United Kingdom.

Then

$$\bar{V} \bar{P} = 73 \times 10^{-3} \times 15 \times 10^{-3}$$
$$= 1095 \times 10^{-6} \text{ where V refers to all violent deaths.}$$

For France $\bar{D}\ \bar{P}^{-1}$ was computed by summing weighted death rates and dividing by 60

$$\bar{D}\ \bar{P}^{-1} = .017$$

We have $\bar{V}\ \bar{D}^{-1} = 96 \times 10^{-3}$

It follows that

$$\begin{aligned}\bar{V}\ \bar{P}^{-1} &= 96 \times 10^{-3} \times 17 \times 10^{-3}\\ &= 1632 \times 10^{-6}\text{ where }\bar{V}\text{ refers to all violent deaths.}\end{aligned}$$

A more exact calculation of ratios (more decimals) is needed to distribute deaths per million population on the separate causes of death so that the total adds up to the marginal total, which gives 1632 with two significant digits (96), but 1636 with five significant digits (96.249). By using three significant digits for the separate causes, the following result is obtained for France 1900—1959.

Cause of death	Deaths per million population per year
Accident	541
Suicide	182
Homicide	18
Hierarchical	3
Territorial, military	709
Territorial, civilian	185
Total	1638

Hence a violence impact corresponding to nearly $\frac{1}{10}$ of all deaths per year 1900—1959 becomes only 1.6 per thousand when related to the average population for the period 1900—1959, which is a quantity about 59 times larger than the annual average number of deaths.

As is seen from the equation above, an increasing death rate means a greater impact of a constant proportion of violent death among all deaths.

Wright (1965, 1942) reported in his Table 57, (p. 665, cf.p. 243 note 64) an estimate necessarily tentative of the number of military deaths in England and France 1600—1930 and related this to an estimate of the average annual number of deaths from all causes.

The results obtained suggest for France a regular increase from 1% of all deaths in the seventeenth century to 6% in the first three decennia of the twentieth century. For England the twentieth century decennia were also the most deadly, but the next most deadly century was reported to be the seventeenth century.

The above demographic account of violent behavior may be compared with a list of deaths stemming from a tribe living in south America around the upper part of the river Orinoco and surviving on primitive agriculture (Chagnon 1968). The account covers 200 «adult» deaths and may be summarized as follows:

Violent deaths	%
Warfare	15
Homicide	1
Accidents[3]	2

Non-violent deaths	
Malaria, epidemics	54
Sorcery[4]	10
Dysentery, Diarrhea	9
Other	9
	100

Because of the practice of infanticide, both male and female, and the expected higher accident risk of children, it does not seem unreasonable that the percentage of violent deaths may well be as high when percent basis is the total number of deaths.

Table 2.2 Violent deaths 1900—1959 in France, Germany, and Russia (USSR) and violent deaths 1901—1960 in the United Kingdom. Absolute figures show thousands (Russia millions) of violent deaths. Relative figures show violent deaths per thousand total deaths in the period

Violent Deaths	United Kingdom		France		Germany		Russia (USSR)	
	Abs.	Rel.	Abs.	Rel.	Abs.	Rel.	Abs.	Rel.
Operational violence:								
Accident	1164	31	1310	32	1633	29	7.61 est.	32 est.
Suicide	279	7	440	11	835	15	2.62 est.	11 est.
Homicide	19	.5	43	1	23	.4	.24 est.	1 est.
Hierarchical violence	1	.03	7	.2	315	6	14	59
Territorial violence:								
War deaths								
Military	1202	32	1720	42	5300	95	12	50
Civilian	64	2	450	11	2550	46	15	63
Total violent deaths	2729	73	3970	96	10656	190	51.472	216
Total deaths	37380		41247		55970		238	

However, it is not known to what extent the results of this investigation are representative of the level of violent deaths found at this stage of technological development.

Notes to Table 2.2

UNITED KINGDOM
The sources used are:
Operational violence
Reports of the Registrar General for England and Wales, Scotland, Northern Ireland, and Ireland.

In addition «Statistical Abstracts» and Mortality Statistics: Accidents and Violence 1975

Hierarchical violence
Data from Ireland 1916, 1917, and Northern Ireland 1921, 1922. The former data weere presented separately, but for the years 1921 and 1922 the homicide figures were inflated. On the sumption that normal operational violence homicides average 10 per year, 1921 and 1922, just like 1923—1930, gave an estimate of 568 rebellion or repression deaths 1921, 1922. Total deaths in Ireland 1916, 1917 due to rebellion were 452.

Territorial violence
Civilian deaths from Statistical Abstracts. Cf. also Hair (1971).
Military deaths from Singer & Small (1972) Tables 4.2 and 4.4.

FRANCE
Operational violence
Accident, suicide, and homicide figures were taken mainly from *Annuaire Statistique Résumé Retrospectif* 1961 and 1966. Missing data were supplemented by interpolations or from Verkko (1951). Accidents 1900—1904 were assumed to have the same total value as accidents 1905—1909. For 1905 the average value of 1906—1909 values was given. Suicides 1900—1905 were taken from Verkko (1951). Values for accidents and suicides 1922—1924 and for 1937—1939 had to be interpolated. The values for the three years 1922—1924 were estimated as three times the average value of the years 1920, 1921, 1925, and 1926. The values for the three years 1937—1939 was estimated as three times the average value for the years 1935—1936.

Homicide statistics were obtained for all 60 years: 1900—1929 from statistics on crimes, and later from the statistics on causes of death. Prior to 1930 Homicides are also included among Accidents *(Annuaire Statistique* 1966 Retrospective volume p. 125). Since homicides constitute such a small part of the total number of accidental deaths, no adjustment was made.

Hierarchical violence
For the years 1930—1960 Tilly (1969) presented figures for the number of internal imbalance situations as well as the average number killed or wounded in each situation. The number killed was estimated by assuming a

1:3.5 ratio between killed and wounded (cf. below section 8.1 on Sorokin's analysis of war). Since the total number estimated as killed 1930—1960 was rather close to the corresponding number for 1830—1860, it seemed defensible to assume a simple doubling of the number killed 1900—1959 compared to 1930—1959. The estimated number killed in internal disturbances became 7299, a very modest number, when compared to other sources of violence during the same period.

Territorial violence
War deaths were obtained from *Annuaire Statistique 1961 Résumé Retrospectif* and from Singer & Small (1972). when these two sources disagreed, the larger value was chosen. World War I civilian deaths were obtained from Chesnais (1976), pp. 178—179). Chesnais estimated the excess civilian mortality at 200,000 for the duration of World War I. He seems to assume that about one-half of this excess mortality is due to the War, because he accepts Huber's and Henry's calculation of military deaths giving 1.4 million military deaths. At the same time Chesnais concludes that total military and civilian losses in World War 1 came to 1.5 million people.

Total deaths
Total deaths were also taken from *Annuaire Statistique Résumé Retrospectif* 1961, 1966, which gives annual averages for five-year periods or some shorter or longer periods which could be multiplied by number of years to give proper subtotals. Deaths taken into account include all deaths, also military deaths, in the period 1900—1959.

GERMANY
Operational violence
Suicides and Accidents were available from the German Statistical Yearbook and from *Statistisches Bundesamt: Bevölkerung und Wirtschaft* 1871—1957.[5] Suicides had to be estimated for the years 1939—1946. For 1939 the average value 1935—1938 var used, together with population 1939, and for 1946 the value for 1947 was assumed.

For the years 1940—1945 the rather regular relationship between German and Swiss suicide values was used by assuming:

German values 1940—1945 = 17.39 times Swiss values 1940—1945. Accident estimates:

> 1914 est. = value for 1913
> 1915—1918 est. = 4 × value 1913
> 1939 est. = 35,000 on the basis of average rise during the previous 4 years.
> 1946—1949 est. = $\frac{4}{5}$ values for 1950—1954
> 1940—1945 est. = (values for 1935—39) × $\frac{6}{5}$ × 1.3[6]

Years for which no acceptable homicide values were found either in Verkko (building on Ferri) or in published and accessible statistics were given homicide values by linear interpolation (1918—22, 1930—33, 1937—48) or by steady state assumption (1956—59).

Hierarchical violence
Relevant numerical data available for the period from Erdmann (1976) gave 313,000, another 1,000 was allowed for the unrest of 1919, and 1,000 for all other internal imbalance deaths.

Territorial violence
Military war deaths stem from Singer & Small and from World War I and World War II, the only two wars Germany participated in during the period studied. The figure for civilian war deaths is that used by Petersen (1961, p. 585).

Total deaths
The sources were *Statistisches Bundesamt, Bevölkerung und Wirtschaft* 1871—1957, and 1872—1972, *Statistisches Jahrbuch*. Total deaths were missing for only years: 1944 and 1945. The value for 1944 was estimated by multiplying population 1944 by death rate observed 1943. The 1945 deaths were estimated as 1/3 (deaths 1944) + 2/3 (deaths 1946).

RUSSIA (USSR)
In order to obtain deaths 1900—1959 for Russia (USSR) it was necessary first to estimate the population within Russian borders for each year in this time interval. The official imperial Russian estimate for 1 January, 1897 was accepted as was also the 1 January, 1914 estimate by USSR authorities.

Since population 1914 = population 1897 times 1.3 235 77, the annual rate of growth is .016 627. By using this rate the Russian population was estimated for 1900—1915. For 1916 and 1917 Volkov's rates were used (cf. Lorimer 1946, Table 12, p. 30). From 1918 to 1927 Volkov's estimates were accepted. From 1928 to 1939 Lorimer's (1946, Table 54, p. 135) figures were accepted. For 1940 and 1941 official estimates were used. thereafter annual decline corresponding to a multiplier of .964301 was used for the years 1942—1945, whereafter a multiplier of 1.00981 was used for the years 1946—1949. For 1950, 1951, 1958 and 1959 Russian official figures were available (Mickiewicz 1973). Between 1952 and 1957 population was estimated by assuming a constant annual multiplier of 1.01741. Death rates were available for 8 of the 12 quinquennial intervals and estimated by linear interpolation for the rest. The sources used were *Annuaire Statistique* 1922, Demographic Yearbook, and The Russian Statistical Yearbook for 1975.

The total number of deaths in Russia 1900—1959 was calculated from death rates and population estimates: 196,558,000. This figure probable includes operational violence and perhaps some deaths from hierarchical and territorial violence. However, it was assumed that hierarchical violence as well as territorial violence 1914—1926 and territorial violence 1941—1945 had not been included in the above sum 196,558,000. For the period 1914—1926 Lorimer (1946) was the authority used, for the period 1941—1945 Eason (1959).

The estimates of the total number of deaths thus increased to 238 millions for the years 1900—1959. Among these it is estimated (Petersen 1961 p. 585) that approx. 15 million civilian died in the Second World War. It was not possible to find estimates for civilian deaths in other wars. Military deaths amounted to 10 million people in World War II alone, according to Petersen[7], whose estimate exceeds Singer & Small's by 2.5 million. In addition, 1,9 million military deaths occurred before and after the second world war, according to Singer & Small. For operational violence the rates observed for France were used, as already mentioned above. The figures in Table 2.2 were rounded off to nearest million. Biraben (1958) worked with different assumptions, and this produced an estimate of total deaths for 1900—1959 of 342.62 millions. [8]With the present author's estimate of violent deaths the proportion of violent deaths is reduced to 150 per thousand. However, it may well be the case that Biraben works with higher estimates of deaths from hierarchical and territoral violence than the present study. If so, the difference in rates would diminish.

2.4 Social Cost of Violent Death

One measure of the social cost of deadly violence is the annual number of deaths which may be related either to all deaths in a year or to the population producing thcsc deaths. This is a first approach to the cost of violence. Let us call it a D-measure of cost. A closer approach is available wherever deaths are tabulated by age and mortality tables show expected years of life remaining for given age. Then a measure of social cost is Y, where Y is defined as follows:

$$Y = \Sigma X_i = \text{years of expected life remaining for age i}$$
$$i = \text{age at death}$$
$$= NX = \text{population times mean expected number of years remaining}$$

Chesnais (1976) computed the Y-measure for males and females separtely and for homicides, suicides, accidental deaths as well as for their sum. The data covered France 1969. He based his study on the cause of death statistics of the Institute National de Sanité et Recherche Medicale, and on Vallin's (1973) study of generational mortality. Persons killed in cases of homicide average 41 years for males and 47 years for females, in cases of suicide 54 years for males and 56 years for females. More striking was the sex difference for accidental death: males 47 years, females 67 years. The average number of expected years of life lost was for all violent deaths 24 for the male sex and 16 for the female sex. As a consequence the total number of years lost due to violent death amounted to 1 million for the single year 1969.

The United States Department of Health produced the Y-measure for all deaths in 1955 among persons aged 20—29.

Altogether 634 thousand man-years were lost from accidental deaths, 73 thousand from suicide, 93 thousand from homicide, and 669 thousand from all other causes of death.

Thus the importance of accidental death in this age category is such that it accounts for about $\frac{4}{10}$ of all years lost from death at age 20—29. (US Dept. of Health 1958, Cf. Norman, 1962).

The change from the D-measure implies that it is no longer, as for D, irrelevant at which age persons are violently killed, because the very young have many years' expectation of life, whereas the very old have few such years and thus the very young deaths contribute relatively more to the total. Still all deaths contribute positively to the Y-measure as well as to the D-measure. This is not generally so if one chooses an economic measure. Reynolds (1956) measured the expected productive value minus the maintenance cost of persons killed in accidents and found as expected that this measure became negative for persons too old to work.

In Dublin's & Lotka's (1930) analysis of the economic value of a man, the first 18 years were taken to be the time needed for making the man productive.

As a consequence the economic value of a man discounted back to birth is less than one-third of the value when the man has arrived at age 26 (assumptions 2500 dollar maximum income ca. 1930 USA, 3 1/2 percent interest). For higher incomes the discrepany becomes considerable larger. Thus with 5000 dollar annual income the maximum present worth of net future earnings (at age 32) is about 5 times the corresponding value for age 0.

3. Operational Violence

«Il suffirait, sans doute, de modifier les
causes qui régissent notre système social,
pour modifier aussi les resultats déplorables
que nous lisons annuellement dans les
annales des crimes et des suicides».

Quételet, A.,
Du systéme social et des lois qui le régissent.
Paris 1848, Guillaumin p. 88.

3.1 Three Causes of Death

The term «operational violence» or steady state violence will be used to refer
to deaths caused by accidents, suicides, and homicides when a social system
operates normally, i.e. is in a steady state, not in a state of imbalance due to
hierarchical violence (revolution, repression, civil disorders) or territorial
violence (war).

Steady state violence may be referred to as the everyday operating cost,
measured in human lives, of the social system. In fact Hair (1971) used the
term «everyday violence» to refer to lethal accidents, suicides, and homicides. The corresponding French expression is «mortalité violente ordinaire».
(See Population 1976, p. 649).

The World Health Organization International classification of diseases,
injuries, and causes of death agreed upon in 1965 and termed the Eighth
Revision classified all causes of death in 17 major categories. The seventeenth and last category is termed «accidents, poisonings, and violence». It is
further subclassified. The most relevant sub-classification for sociological use
is the E 17 or external cause classification. Its main subcategories are:

Transport accidents
Poisonings
Falls
Fires
Other accidents
Suicide
Homicide
Legal intervention
War
Injury undetermined whether due to accidents, suicide, or homicide

Several of the accident categories are further subdivided (6 subdivisions for transport accidents, 3 for poisonings). The «other accidents» category includes accidents due to drowning, and accidents due to firearms. A variety of accidents mainly occurring in industrial work are also included.

Natural disasters also belong here (World Health Organization 1967, 1969). For a discussion of the lethal toll of the major disasters see Thygerson (1977).

For years without war the tripartition accidents, suicide, and homicide take care of the vast majority of deaths classified in the seventeenth category of the Eighth revision of the International Classification of death.

For the calculation performed in section 2.3 the deaths due to legal intervention (executions etc.), if known, were added to the homicides. The final undetermined category, if known, was placed among accidents as the most likely category.

The seven earlier classifications were dated respectively 1955, 1948, 1938, 1929, 1920, 1909 and 1900.

In England and Wales 1975 there were 12,274 male deaths for each million males in the population. The four major causes (Int. Class. Eight Rev. 1965) of death were:

Male deaths per 10^6 1975 male population	
1) Diseases of the circulatory system	6101
2) Neoplasms	2769
3) Diseases of the respiratory system	1832
4) Accidents, poisonings, and violence	486

(Office of Population Censuses Series DH2 No. 2 Mortality 1975 England and Wales).

It will be seen that operational violence deaths are the fourth most important cause of male deaths in England and Wales 1975.

Among the three types of violent deaths normally distinguished under operational violence, accidents are by far the most important contributor to the death toll.

Thus in 1970 the USA had 763 deaths per million population due to accidents, suicides, and homicides, but the special rates differed: for all accidents it was 564 per million, for suicides 116, and for homicides 83 per million. In 1900 the corresponding rates were:

Total rate	837
Accidents	723
Suicides	102
Homicides	12

In modern times motor accidents are a major type of deadly accidents. Their rate per million was 269 in the USA in 1970.

If it is reasonable to see these deaths from accidents, suicides, and homicides as part of the operating costs of a social system, then it might be likely to observe positive correlations among the three types of death because of a component common to all three.

If the common component is strong enough not to be suppressed by factors not shared by the three varieties of operational violence, then one should expect a positive set of correlation between the three mortality rates. A study by Porterfield (1960) gave precisely this result.

He documented that an index of motor traffic deaths was related to homicide ($r = .6$), to suicide ($r = .5$), and to their sum ($r = .7$).

For the states of the USA he likewise documented a positive relationship between homicides + suicides and an index of deaths per 10^8 passenger miles ($r = .7$).[1] The cited r's are for white males, white females showed a weaker relationship among the variables.

A corroboration of the positive intercorrelations came from Whitlock's international study (cf. below sec. 3.4).

One common factor is the frequent finding that alcohol is partly involved in all three main variants of operational violence (cf. below sec. 3.5). A more basic common factor which Whitlock hypothetically inferred from his study was a pervasive aggressive drive. Henry & Short (1954) had already assumed tentatively that homicide and suicide were alike in the sense that they were both «aggressive reactions to frustrations».

Certain places of death create greater uncertainty about the cause of death than others. Thus bath-tub deaths are difficult to classify because they could be due to accident, or suicide or homicide, and they may even be due to non-violent causes of death. Geertinger & Voigt (1969) stressed this indetermination as a motive for their study of 42 cases of bath-tub deaths in Copenhagen and Gothenburg. The cases were found among the deaths occurring in these two cities 1961—1968.

The majority of cases were diagnosed as suicides (30/42). Only 9 cases were defined as natural deaths (4) or accidental deaths (5). The remaining three cases were certain homicides (1) or probable homicides (2).

3.2 Trend

Hair tried to compare the death tolls from operational violence over the past 500 years of British history and arrived at the conclusion that such violence «has almost certainly not increased over the centuries and probably declined». However, his conclusion must be deemed highly tentative, since reliable, nationwide statistics do not cover much more than the period since 1830.

The total number of everyday violence deaths per million per year was about 500 in the 1960s and 800 in the 1860s. Thereupon the sources become less adequate. If it may be assumed that the corresponding number for earlier centuries is unlikely to be less than the figure for the nineteenth century, then one may conclude as the author does.

His own figures for various regions of England c. 1500 — c. 1800 are in general lower than the figure for 1860, but figures from the earlier period *may* be underestimates.

The suicide rate in the United Kingdom 1901—1970 has been tending towards a steady state of about 100 suicides per million population. Values in the distant past are either unavailable or of unknown but probably low reliability due to underestimation. Homicide is a very rare event unable to affect the total rate of operational violence much. It follows that Hair's hypothesis depends primarily on the changes observed in the rate of fatal accidents. (See separate trend discussions for accidents, suicides, and homicides in the following sections).

3.3 Risk Customs and Operational Cost

It should be emphatically stated that the term operational violence or steady state violence is in no way used to imply that a social system is bound to have a certain degree of such violence regardless of safety measures. Rather it is suggested that the operative procedures of the system are increasingly risky, wasteful and costly the more lives are violently ended.

Even if it is assumed that the aggressiveness of the human animal is such as to make some violence unavoidable, there does not seem to be any good theory that would imply that such violence has to be lethal or that it was necessary to sacrifice as many lives as actually was the case.

Jacobziner (1957) reported on an investigation of 3000 children in New York, all victims of non-fatal accidents. The children were mostly (about 90%) in the age-group 1/2 — 5 years of age. The two most frequent accidents were burns and falls. Jacobziner concluded after a detailed investigation of the sample that 90% of the accidents were preventable. In particular he noted a lack of adult supervision at the time and place of accidental occurrence. He also reported on a special investigation of 1151 cases of fatal and non-fatal poisoning among children under 15 years and concluded that 98% of accidental poisonings were preventable. In regard to child accidents in general an inverse relationship with social class was observed: the lower the class, the higher the accident rate. Boys are more frequently hit by accidents than girls. Lack of knowledge is a more important factor than carelessness.

Jacobziner stressed that accidents are predictable. «With a certain constellation of circumstances, an injurious agent, a susceptible host and an unsafe environment, an accidental occurrence will inevitably result».

Dalgård (1961) noted that Denmark had one carbon monoxide (CO) death per day and added that most of them could have been avoided with proper precaution.

Norman (1962) in a review of road accidents wrote that the great majority of road accidents were preventable.

According to Bull (1975) prevention of accidents has been summarized as Education, Engineering, and Enforcement. Bull noted a recent trend in education for accident prevention: positive training has received increased emphasis as against exhortation or admonition. engineering inventions may provide a safer environment of tools, machinery, vehicles, etc. so as to reduce the accident rate both in transport, in industry, and in the home. Enforcement may aid in accident prevention to the extent that enforcement is socially accepted or at least tolerated by the population.

However, it may well be the case that society will continue to be dangerous and that this characteristic is too closely tied to basic industrial technology to be easily changed.

Chesnais (1976, p. 277) emphasized that operational violence is distinguished from other causes of death because: «Plus que toute autre cause de mort, la mort violente est en effet sous la dependence trés etroite du comportement humain, donc du milieu social et des habitudes de risque ou de vigilance qui lui sont propres . . .»

It is possible to view the present accident mortality as part of the price to be paid for the speed, regularity, and individual autonomy characterizing modern social systems. Sauvy's comment on transport companies and their accident rates may probably be generalized: «Il serait possible d'éviter à peu pres tout accident, en prenant les précautions necessaires. Mais au delà d'un certain degré ces efforts ne seraient plus payants et se traduiraient par des dépenses trop élevées ou par des pertes de recettes resultant de la moindre vitesse ou de la moindre regularité. L'expérience et les calculs conduisent a une mortalité optimale mais ces resultats ne gagnent pas a être précisés ni surtout publiés» (Sauvy1956, pp. 346—7).

3.4 Aggressive Customs

Whitlock (1971) suggested that violent death by accident, by suicide or by homicide as well as non-homicidal violent crimes be looked upon «as manifestation of the quality and quantity of aggression in a given society».

The build-up of aggressiveness as one passes from normal behavior off the road to automotive behavior seemed to Whitlock to make sense only if one assumes an aggressive drive strong enough to overcome rational restraint.

Empirically Whitlock assembled data for 27 nations and 47 American states around 1960 which made it possible to assess correlates and predictors of road deaths. Thus in his international study he observed the following correlates of accidental road deaths:

1) Total other accidental deaths   .51
2) Homicide   .22
3) Suicide   .46
4) Sum 1 + 2 + 3   .54
5) Forcible rape   .71
6) Robbery   .51
7) Total violent crime   .61
8) Drunken driving   .41
9) Male deaths from cirrhosis of the liver[2]   .49

Whitlock found that the distribution of accidents by sex, by age, and by social class, i.e. the predominance of young males of lower social class in accidents, tended to support the view that road behavior is at least in part determined by an aggressive drive leading to defence of territory, in this case a person's own car, which could well mean more to a young male of lower class than to any other category defined by sex, age, and social status only.

Whitlock concluded that the results of his investigation «in general terms» supported the initial hypothesis: that road violence is one aspect of social violence and that the higher the incidence of such intrasocial aggression becomes, the higher will be the rates for deaths and injuries onthe roads. Aggression was not seen as the only factor causing road deaths. The road user's health condition, his alcohol behavior, and the condition of the vehicle were in particular mentioned.

Chesnais calculated the proportion of all annual deaths in a sex-age category which were due to deaths by operational violence (accidents, suicides, homicides) and found the highest proportion 1931—33 in the male age categories 15—29, where the proportion of all deaths due to operational violence ranged from .188 to .203. These sex-age categories were also dominant in 1968—70, but at this time the general mortality had gone down, whereas the operational violence rates had increased slightly for males and doubled for females.

The result for the male age category 15—29 was that operational violence now accounted for from 65 to 74% of the deaths in the age interval.

3.5 Alcohol Customs

Alcohol consumption is related to all three types of operational violence: accidents, suicides, and homicides. Alcohol is thus a factor tending to make the death toll from operational violence higher (Cp. Chesnais 1976, p. 277).

In New York city all «sudden, medically unattended, traumatic or potentially unnatural deaths», including all deaths from accident, suicide, homicide, drug addiction, and alcohol intoxication are investigated by a Chief Medical Examiner. Haberman & Baden (1974) analyzed one thousand cases and found 297 alcoholics. The alcoholics constituted of course 100% of the group certified as having died from alcoholism. In addition the alcoholics constituted rather exactly 25% of those certified as having died from accidents, homicide, and drug addiction, and they constituted 9% of the suicide cases.

A study in Vermont prepared by Waller for the American violence commission of 1968 showed that persons causing firearms accidents were also more involved than others in traffic accidents, criminal violence, and heavy drinking (Newton & Zimring 1969, p. 29).

Reigstad et al. (1977) investigated the occurrence of alcohol in the blood of 616 persons of 15 years of age and older who visited a hospital clinic for primary treatment because of accidents. The investigation took place in Oslo, Norway, during the week starting at 8 a.m. on 29. October 1973. Among these 616 accident patients 119 or 19% had alcohol in the blood. The majority had a concentration between .50 and 2.99 g/l but no less than 18 or 16% had 3.00 g/l or more. Among the days of the week Saturday had the highest frequency of accidents with intoxication in this sample, and the time between 23 and 07 was in the same sense the most dangerous.

Alcohol concentration was rather low for work accidents and sport accidents and very high for a kind of accident termed «violence» by the authors. It seems to include all cases of maltreatment of men by men.

The authors concluded that the accident rate might be reduced by reducing the consumption of alcohol.

Zylman (1974) estimated that 36% of 56,600 motor vehicle deaths in the United States 1972 « may have involved alcohol in some causal fashion». He stressed that most traffic deaths (64% or more) must be caused by factors other than alcohol.

Straus (1976) seems to accept another and higher estimate of alcohol-related motor vehicle deaths bringing the relative proportion of such deaths in the United States up to one-half of all highway deaths. In OECD (1978) it is estimated that «approximately 45%» of dead drivers in North America 1972—1973 had more than .8 g/l alcohol in their bodies at the time of the fatal accident.

Chesnais & Vallin (1977, p. 1249) reported on a recent study of lethal accidents in France conducted at the hospital Raymond-Poincaré de Garches in which 38% of the persons responsible for lethal accidents had a level of alcohol in the blood exceeding the legal limit of .8 gram per liter.

England and Wales, which have the same legal limit, had 36% of fatal accident drivers exceeding this limit as of 1975 (OECD 1978).

Studies of samples of the driving population of the Western World in the 1970s suggest that at most 15% have .5 g/l or more alcohol concentration in the blood (ibid p. 24).

Thygerson (1977, p. 128) reported on a study by Perrine in Vermont. In this study it was inferred that one-half of all drivers at fault in fatal crashes came from those 2% of the driving population who had been drinking heavily.

Goldberg (1970) reviewed research on alcohol and traffic risk and concluded that all three methods used — laboratory experiments, field studies, and accident investigations — document that alcohol consumption reduces driving competence and increases the risk of accidents. In particular he noted that alcohol was a more important risk factor in lethal traffic accidents than in non-lethal accidents.[3].

The reduction of driving competence seemed to start with about .5 g/l alcohol in the blood.

Laurell (1977) reported on the basis of realistic driving experiments that the results gave clear evidence of the degrading effects of alcohol on driving performance in emergency situations. These detrimental effects were found to exist at blood alcohol concentrations below .5 g/l; the overall mean blood alcohol content was .42 g/l. Thus this research could be considered a corroberation of earlier research (Bjerver & Goldberg 1950, *Quart. J. Studies on Alcohol* 11:1—30) in which impairment of driving was documented at .48 g/l blood alcohol concentration.

According to Pærregaard (1963), most studies report 10—30% alcoholists among suicide cases. In her own material for the municipality of Copenhagen 1951—1955, with a suicide rate of 410 per million per year, she found 43% misusers of alcohol among her male sample (N = 955) and 11% in her female sample (N = 515). Overconsumption of medicin without alcoholism characterized 3% of the males and 10% of the females.

Retterstöl (1971, p. 73) reported suicidal frequencies among alcoholic and medicinal overconsumers in Oslo, Norway. The frequencies were from 60 to 80 times normal suicidal frequencies. He also reported other studies tending to find from 5% to 8% suicidal deaths among alcoholics or from 50 000 to 80 000 per million.

In Wolfgang's study of homicide no measurement of the alcohol consumption of offenders was available, but police officers had simply entered their impressions and information received as to the presence of alcohol. In 588 homicide cases 44% were characterized as cases where alcohol was present in both victims and offender. In another 20% only one of the parties had consumed alcohol. As a consequence the majority of cases were stated to be influenced by alcohol; only 36% of the homicides took place in the absence of alcohol, provided these observations are trustworthy. Hansen's measurements (1977) gave considerably lower figures. He found that 18% of the offenders and 27% of the victims in his homicide material were estimated to have a concentration of alcohol in the blood equal to or exceeding .5 g/l.

Pernanen, who recently (1976) reviewed the evidence for the relationship between alcohol use and violent behavior, concluded that «prolonged, excessive» alcohol use (not further delimited) was connected with a higher risk of displaying violent behavior. Lint & Schmidt (1976) suggested that the excessive daily dosis would frequently be defined as 15 centiliters of pure alcohol or more per day. Like so many other variables under social influence, alcohol use reveals an approximately lognormal distribution. This means that most people are non-drinkers or modest drinkers. But a few percent of the population account for a large part of the total quantity of alcohol consumed (cf. Lint & Schmidt 1976).

Ledermann (1956—1964) documented that the French male death rates from cirrhosis of the liver and from alcoholism for the year 1955 and the age category 15—54 years were both very high (450 per million) among unskilled workers and both very low among middle level administrative personnel («cadres moyens» 130 and 30) and among the liberal professions and upper level administrative personnel (100 and 10). In regard to cirrhosis of the liver seamen and fishermen came rather close to the rate among unskilled workers. So far the Ledermann data present a picture of lower class preponderance in alcoholism.

However, there are certain categories that seemingly deviate from this pattern. Thus merchants and shopkeepers («commercants»), employers in industry and commerce, craftsmen and manufacturers also had very high cirrhosis rates.

There is thus a clear documentation of differences in alcohol-conditioned death rate by profession. In this study the indicators seemed to point towards a lower class preponderance in alcoholism.

In contrast the Swedish 1968 Low Income investigations pointed rather consistently to the top 8 percent of the Swedish population as the largest consumers of alcohol. (Johansson 1970).

Data for England and Wales 1970—1972 documented that mortality for cirrhosis of the liver[4] was higher than expected on the basis of age distribution in all the three highest social classes and in the lowest social class. The classification used altogether six classes.

Among occupations with the highest mortality from cirrhosis of the liver were publicans, innkeepers, hotel and boardinghouse proprietors and managers, finance and/or insurance brokers, financial agents, restaurateurs, authors, journalists, medical practictioners, and garage proprietors, all or most of them occupations probably above average either in regard to prestige or in regard to income (Office of Population Censuses and Surveys 1978).

Boalt & von Euler (1959) reported on a survey on alcohol consumption undertaken by the Swedish Central Statistical Office 1955. A graph presenting the findings in summary form showed that several measures of consumption revealed a curvilinear shape, with the middle class as the lowest alcohol consumer.

A study in Denmark 1976 executed by the Danish National Institute for Social Research documented that the highest stratum among those employed were most likely to report drinking the equivalent of 1 liter beer or more per day (6%). among the unemployed the corresponding percentage was 10%, again a suggestion of a curvilinear relationship (Geckler, S. et al. 1978).

The author is tempted to conclude that alcoholism is curvilinearly related to social status. There is more of it towards the extremes of status while the middle layers seem better fitted for survival.

The importance of drugs in traffic accidents cannot be established at present, because of the difficulties involved in measuring drug concentration in the organism and the limited knowledge on the relationship between drug effects and road accident risk. It is possible that the main effect of drugs may be found among drinking drivers and thus contribute to the seriousness of accidents perhaps more often than to the number of accidents (cf. OECD 1978). The same source noted a growing use of cannabis in North America.

Alcohol customs may also help explain the high level of mortality from accidents observed or inferred for the middle of the nineteenth century and earlier.

Fekjær (1980, p. 95) suggested an equation which assumes a rather automtic relatinship between alcohol consumption and mortality from alcohol in a nation; for constant proportion adults (15 years or older) in the population as follows:

$$D = kAPP_a^{-1} \cdot 10^{-6}$$

where: D = number of deaths conditioned by alcohol

$\quad\quad$ k = a constant = 65 ± 5

$\quad\quad$ A = total alcohol consumption in liters per year

$\quad\quad$ P = total population

$\quad\quad$ P_1 = population aged 15 years or more

Thus France had about 53 million inhabitants in 1977. Among these 41 million were 15 years old or more.

Assume $\frac{A}{P} = 20$ or an average of 20 liters consumption per capita.

Then we may write

$$D = 65 \, (20 \cdot 53 \cdot 10^6) \frac{53}{41} \, 10^{-6}$$

$$= 65 \cdot 20 \cdot 53 \cdot 1.29 = 88881$$

or around 90,000 deaths, which is a recent estimate of the number of deaths caused by alcohol.

Swedish customs as outlined by Bruun (1973) can not be too far from the European average.

Around 1500 food consisted to a large extent of dried or salted meat or fish — not always tasty. This explains the relatively high level of beer consumption (the only alcoholic liquor of importance at that time in Sweden). Historians estimate an annual consumption of 1500 liters beer per capita. It is generally assumed that the beer was weak, but even with only 2% alcohol the annual consumption per capita becomes 30 liters pure alcohol. The consumption seems to have remained high up to c. 1850. In the meantime strong liquor had been added to the diet and c. 1820 the consumption of aquavite alone is estimated at 40 liters per capita, corresponding to approx. 20 liters pure alcohol. In the course of the nineteenth century a decline[5] in alcohol consumption began which reached as low consumption per year and inhabitant as 3.0 to 3.5 liters in the period 1920—1945.

After 1945 consumption started to rise and had not reached a turning point by 1972 (Finnish Foundation, International Statistics, 1977).

The chances of reducing the heavy load of operational violence by reducing alcohol consumption do not appear to be good at the present time. Statistics from most European — North-American nations revealed a trend of increasing consumption of alcohol in the period covered by the International Statistics edited by the Finnish Foundation for Alcohol Studies (1950—1972). Steady state or decline in per capita consumption was only noted for some of the wine-growing European Countries (France, Italy, Portugal, Romania, Greece).

Moderate increase corresponding at most to doubling in 20 years or annual relative increase of 3.5% characterized USA, Canada, United Kingdom, Ireland, Sweden, Norway, Luxembourg, Switzerland, Spain, Hungary, Poland and USSR:

Higher rates of growth characterized the two Germanies, Austria, and several of their neighbors: Danmark, Netherlands, Czechoslovakai, Yugoslavia, Bulgaria, Finland.

3.5 Marital Status and Sex

Peller (1965) expressed himself rather categorically to the effect that married men are better risks than bachelors. His study of 8500 members of Europe's ruling families since 1500 showed that bachelors had higher mortality, age constant, up to age 39 for those born 1480—1679 and to age 44 for those born 1680—1879.

American statistics on death rates from motor vehicle accidents 1949—1951 documented that married males, regardless of age if 20 years or more, were less exposed to death from motor vehicle accidents than were either single males or widowed or divorced males. The difference was quite marked, the rate coming nearest to the one for married males was normally twice as high or higher. (United States Department of Health. Accidental Injury Statistics Washington D.C. 1958. Here cited from Norman 1962). Females seemed in general to be better protected by avoiding the marital state, the widowed state, and the divorced state altogether, although the differences were small for them between the single and the married.

The advantage of the single or married female state as against the two others were highest in the younger years and tended in general to level off from age 45 on.

At least since Durkheim the importance of marriage as a life-preserving factor and hence a protection against suicide has been noted and repeatedly documented.

Laerum et al.(1979) documented for Denmark 1972 the suicide protection afforded by the married state and discovered that the most suicidal marital category was those persons who were in the process of becoming divorced (separated persons).

In France 1968—79 important differences according to marital state and suicide were observed. Widowers were age constant the most suicidal category among males, next came unmarried persons, then divorced persons, while married males were best protected against suicide. A similar pattern appeared among females, but the differences observed over marital categories were much smaller. (Chesnais 1976 pp. 82—83).

For the USA 1940, Henry & Short (1954, p. 137) likewise documented the advantage of the married state.

Demographic studies published 1967—70 by the National Center of Health statistics demonstrated again and rather convincingly the superior protection given in the United States by marriage in regard to risk of dying from motor accident, suicide, and homicide on the basis of statistics for the years 1959—61. Not only is the married state the most favored state in terms of survival in all the three causes of death, but the three other states follow each other in unchanging rank order regardless of cause of death (among the three causes mentioned). (The single state comes next in safety regardless of cause, followed by widowed. The divorced state was the least favored, with a chance of motor accident death and of suicide more than 3 times of the married state, and a doubled chance of being killed by homicide. (see Table 3.5).

The same institution documented also for the USA 1959—61 that the protection of the marital state even extended to many numerically important, non-violent causes of death. The most dramatic change in mortality risk was noted for cirrhosis of the liver, where the rate among the divorced was more than 6 times that among the married.

In fact Ledermann (1964, p. 95) documented that for each sex and age category (12 age categories for each sex) the married had invariantly the lower mortality rate in France 1953—54.

The male sex is more likely to die from operational violence than the female sex. This generalization holds for accidents, for suicide, and usually also for homicide. The explanation should probably be sought partly in the difference between the masculine value hierarchy and the feminine value hierarchy, partly in the differential allocation of males and females in the occupational structure. Masculine values typically include a higher emphasis on aggressive behavior, and males are typically more often placed in the more risky occupational categories and do in general more often undertake risky pursuits.

3.7 Social Class

Social class is related to operational violence. Data for England and Wales 1970—72 documented in general a deficit of operational violence in the upper four classes and a surplus in the lower two classes. (Office of Population Censuses 1978). The available findings usually agree on the lower class over-representation in regard to accidents and in regard to homicide (murderers and victims). In regard to suicide European and some American data give the same picture of lower class over-representation. Other American studies report a proponderance of suicides in the upper and middle strata.

A few studies report a curvilinear tendency in the relationship between operational violence and social class to the effect that the risk is relatively larger at the extremes of the class or statushierarchy.

The middle strata are probably more characterized by the dominance of norms of security, of the value of life, and in general may be ideologically more protected against operational violence than others. The curvilinear relationship is consequently a highly plausible finding. This curvilinear tendency may be hard to discover, even if it is present, because the upper status categories are hard to discover or isolate in samples of conventional size or in classifications of conventional number of categories.

For accidents the lower class proponderance is convincingly demonstrated with French data from 1955—65 by Chesnais 1976, p. 119, Table 38). The accident death rate per million population among males aged 35—44 years is for unskilled workers 1690, but for the Catholic clergy 400 and for teachers only 280. The average was 910 (cf. also *Danmarks Statistik* 1979).

Sowby (1965) computed death risk per 10^9 hours of exposure and per individual for certain occupations assuming 2000 hours annual work time. He used English data 1949—53 for males aged 20—64. He partly confirmed Chesnais by showing the occupational risks of coal miners and fishermen to be more than five times as high as those for medical practitioners. At the same time there was a suggestion of a great range of risk among high-ranking occupations. Thus while the death risk per 10^9 occupant or worker hours was only 60 for physicians and radiologists, it was computed to be 675 for construction engineers and 2500 for airline crew-members. Horse-racing and professional boxing were still more risky.

In regard to suicide the curvilinear finding could be documented for France 1961—65, for England and Wales 1949—53 and for Denmark 1956, and 1972 (Chesnais 1976, p. 79, Dublin 1963, Rudfeld 1962, Laerum et al. 1979).

Laerum et al. documented the curvilinear relatinship between suicide and social status both for males and for females. In both sexes the risk of suicide were at a minimum among the 30 percent of the Danish population defined as lower middle class and largest in the most extreme classes: the top approx. 5% stratum and the bottom approx. 20% stratum.

A simple linear relationship with the lower class values at the top was reported for France 1955—65 for both of two male age categories (Chesnais 1976, Table 28, p. 80).

Thus for males aged 45 to 55 the rate of suicide among unskilled workers was 790 per million population while the rate for higher administrators and liberal professions was 130.

American studies invariably document a class factor in suicides committed in the United States but the studies arrive at seemingly contradictory findings as to the more suicide-prone class location:

Lalli & Turner (1968), using 1950 US data, found that white suicides were more frequent the lower the social class, hence confirming Chesnais' finding.

Non-white suicides did not vary much by social class. Hackney (1969), who used 1940 data, reported significant and *positive* correlations of size .5—.6 between suicide and respectively education, income, and wealth for white Americans and a similar although weaker relationship for non-whites.

Humphry & Kupferer (1977) confirmed Hackney's finding by reporting high status proponderance of suicides in North Carolina.

It may well be that more comprehensive investigations would reveal a curvilinear relationship with the middle locations as the best protected.

In regard to homicide a lower class preponderance has been repeatedly documented (Wolfgang 1958, 1968, Hansen 1977, Hackney 1969, Lalli & Turner 1968, Humphry & Kupferer 1977). Siciliano (1965) seems to be the first study that documented a curviliniar tendency even for homicide.

Siciliano located the offenders within the nine strata used by Svalastoga (1959) and found the following distribution of offenders in Denmark 1933—61:

	Number of offenders	Offenders per million inhabitants in given strata
Upper strata (1—4)	23	7
Middle strata (5,6)	97	2
Working class strata (7,8)	404	6
Lowest stratum (9)	29	71
Stratum unknown	27	

It will be seen that the typical working class strata (skilled and unskilled manual workers and occupations similar in prestige to these) do not relatively recruit more killers than the uppr strata, but produce killers with three times the probability of the middle classes. The main relative overproducers of killers seem to be the bottom stratum containing stigmatized occupatins and persons with reduced freedom og movement. Some uncertainty remains because the size of this stratum was difficult to estimate (Svalastoga 1959).

Because of the repeatedly documented strong tendency of homicidal criminals to choose their victims primarily within their own group of family relatives, friends, and acquaintances it is necessary to conclude that the victims will show the same distribution by class as the criminals.

Table 3.1 England and Wales 1901—1974. Death from Operational violence. Annual average death rate per million population

Years	Total rate	Accident rates Road transport	Other*	Suicide rate	Homicide rate
1901—05	591	75	405	101	9
1906—10	554	70	373	102	8
1911—15	578	90	368	96	8
1916—20	605	108	329	85	7
1921—25	449	82	257	101	6
1926—30	534	144	260	123	6
1931—35	548	158	248	135	5
1936—40	712	162	288	123	4
1941—45	821	139	274	92	5
1946—50	446	101	230	106	5
1951—55	456	108	237	107	4
1956—60	495	128	234	116	5
1961—65	514	148	244	116	6
1966—70	483	144	239	93	7
1970—74		340**			

* Includes cases, except for 1980—74 entry, that as of 1961 and later were labelled «doubtful whether accidental or purposeful». Office of Population. Mortality Statistics England and Wales DH4 nr. 2 Table 1, London, 1977. 1970—1974 from World Health Statistics Annual 1978.
** Roadtransport + Other

Table 3.2 France 1826—1974. Death from Operational violence. Annual average death rate per million population

Years	Accidents	Suicides	Homicides	Total operational violence
1826—30	230	47	12	289
1831—35	248	57	13	318
1836—40	295	68	11	374
1841—45	345	76	11	432
1846—50	375	87	12	474
1851—55	382	90	10	482
1856—60	436	98	8	542
1861—65	488	110	7	605
1866—69	543	121	7	671
1872—75	511	134	8	653
1876—80	509	151	8	668
1881—85	530	173	9	712
1886—90	488	193	9	690
1891—95	500	215	9	724
1896—00	491	212	8	711
1901—05	454	204	8	666
1906—10	466	217	11	694
1911—13	502	225	11	738
1920—21	480	189	13	681
1926—30*	504	192	8	703
1931—35	493	205	11	709
1940—45		140		
1946—50	486	137	8	631
1951—55	565	157	6	728
1956—60	607	165	17	789
1961—65	666	152	12	831
1966—70	767	155	8	922
1970—74	758			

Source: Chesnais 1976. Various Tables 1970—74.
World Health Statistics, Annual 1978.

* *Suicide and Homicide: 1928—29.*

Table 3.3 USA 1901—1974. Death from Operational violence. Annual average death rate per million population

Years	Accidents	Suicides	Homicides
1901—05	809	115	14
1906—10	870	151	45
1911—15	797	159	58
1916—20	780	121	67
1921—25	719	119	81
1926—30	784	138	85
1931—35	756	159	91
1936—40	764	146	70
1941—45	728	112	55
1946—50	654	114	58
1951—55	594	102	48
1956—60	539	103	46
1961—65	532	108	50
1966—70	573	110	72
1970—74	542		

Source: 1901—1970 Annual rates given in Historical Statistics.
1970—1974 World Health Statistics. Annual 1978.

Table 3.4 Sweden 1761—1974. Death from Operational violence. Annual average death rate per million population

Years	Accidents	Suicides	Homidicides	Total
1761—70			7	
1771—80			6	
1781—90		22	7	
1791—00		25	6	
1801—10		33	7	
1811—20		42	8	
1821—30		59	11	
1831—40		63	14	
1841—50		67	16	
1851—60	491	63	17	571
1861—70	512	82	20	614
1871—80	489	87	22	598
1881—90	437	103	16	556
1891—00	434	127	20	581
1901—10	388	151	15	554
1911—20	398	146	13	557
1921—30	343	148	9	500
1931—40	383	163	8	554
1941—45	389	147	8	544
1946—50	374	148	7	529
1951—55	394	170	7	571
1956—60	400	181	7	588
1961—65	444	185	7	636
1966—70	431	216	8	655
1970—74	445			

Source:
1761—1850 mean of quinquennial medians based on Verkko (1951).
1851—1945 Historisk Statistik för Sverige, Statistisk översigtstabel Stockholm 1960 Table 143.
Rates were obtained by dividing observed values by population defined as $\frac{1}{2}(P_0 + P_1)$ where 0 and 1 refer to beginning and end of period. 1946—70:

Medians of annual rates. Other sources used were Dödsorsaker, Statistisk Årsbok. 1971—74: World Health Statistics Annual 1978.

Table 3.5 USA 1959—1961. Marital Status and Death from Operational Violence. Age-adjusted mortality rates per 100,000 population. (Age 15 and over, both sexes, whites and non-whites). Annual average

Marital status	Motor vehicle accident	Suicide	Homicide
All marital states	27.4	14.0	6.6
Single	37.0	20.9	10.7
Married	21.8	11.9	5.4
Widowed	56.8	23.8	19.9
Divorced	66.9	39.9	21.5

(National Center for Health Statistics Series 20 Numbers 5.6, and 9. Washington D.C. 1967, and Rockville Md. 1970).

4. Accident

4.1 Trend

Reliable and nationally representative figures for deaths by accident may be hard to find prior to c. 1860. The most likely explanation for data given in Table 3.2 for France 1826—1860 is that recording deficiencies have caused many fatal accidents to remain unregistered (cf. Chesnais 1976, p. 108).

For the following one hundred and ten years up to about 1950 there seems to have been a general trend in the Western world towards a decreasing rate of mortality from accidents. This is documented for France, Sweden, and England (Hair 1971) from about 1860, and for USA from about 1900.

Then followed a general increase in the rate of accidents documented by World Health statistics (Annual 1978) on the continent of Europe, both for

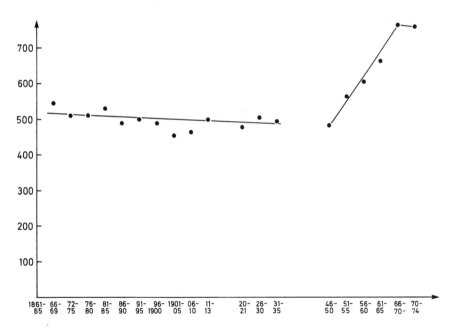

Fig. 4.1 France 1861 – 1974. Fatal accidents per million population. Data from Table 3.2.

France, Germany, and Italy; England too had a modest increase up to about 1965, whereas the American accident rate continued its downward trend.

A partial explanation for this increase in Europe is the great expansion in the number of private cars in Western Europe since 1950, and the simultaneous rise in the number killed on the roads. This factor should be expected to be more lethal on the European continent than in England, because a higher traffic density is likely on the main continental European roads than on English roads.

It is also reasonable to expect higher figures in or close to the central areas of Western Europe (Germany and France) than on its perifery (e.g. Scandinavia).

The increase in accident mortality in Europe c. 1950—c. 1975 was not limited to motor vehicle accidents, but comprised also that important subcategory of accidents labelled «Falls». Falls killed 72 persons per million in France 1950—55, but 242 persons per million 1970—74 and was in that quinquennium as important as road deaths in France.

The central importance of falls among accidents may have become strengthened over the last c. 150 years because of the increase in the average age of the population.[1] The widespread increase in the accident rate during the first 20—25 years after World War II seemed to shift into a steady state or decline around 1970.

It is probably significant that both West Germany, France, and USA reached a maximum rate of *traffic deaths* in the years 1969—72, and Great Britain and Sweden similarly peaked around 1965 (see Vallin & Chesnais 1975).

In fact the OECD report (1978) noted a downward trend in the OECD area amounting to a 15% reduction of road deaths in the course of the period 1973—77.

A formal trend analysis of the English data 1901—1970 gave a correlation coefficient of $-.90$ between Accidents and Time, since the two variables had variances of approximately the same magnitude $b_{AT} = -.90$. $N = 14$. It may be added that the values so far observed for England 1971 and later have been close to the minimum values observed 1901—1970.

The author tends to consider a descending trend in accidents as the most plausible long-term hypothesis for industrialized and urbanized nations, because it seems likely that accidents will be increasingly predictable and consequently, even if with some delay, controllable. Such control is a value that will have to compete with other values, and control may not always prove the more strongly held value. But even in the field of evaluation the force of rationality may well lead to more stress on safety and to less emphasis than now on an individual's right to live dangerously.

Accidental death depends upon scientific and technological development, but the net effect of this force may well be severely damped. Although some accidents become next to impossible (well-drowning) new accidents (aircraft crashes) become possible. More important is the serious lag in the development of the social sciences and of social technologies.

4.2 Death Toll

Accidental death occur during the normal operations of the social system. Four activity areas account for most accidents:

1. Transport
2. Work
3. Home
4. Recreation

Data for the USA for the year 1956 (Haddon et al. 1956, pp. 32—33) showed that Transport was the main killer, taking 45,000 lives, Home the next with 26,000 lives, Work followed with 14,000 lives, and recreation with 11,000 lives. Some indicators of the annual cost of accidents in the USA for the periode 1963—1965 were:

Persons killed	104,000
Working years of life lost	2,000,000
Persons injured	52,000,000
Bed-disabled	11,000,000
Having received medical care	45,000,000
Hospitalized	2,000,000
Days of restricted activity	512,000,000
Days of bed-disability	132,000,000
Days of work loss	90,000,000
Days of school loss	11,000,000
Hospital bed-days	22,000,000

For each person killed there were about 500 persons injured (Iskrant & Joliet 1968).[2]

From a Danish middle-sized (approx. 100,000 inhabitants) city Jensenius (1957) reported on one year's accident treatment 1954—55. There were 12,745 accidents, of which 67 proved to be fatal and another 2,000 needed hospitalization, but the vast majority, approx. 11,000, were able to leave the hospital at once, although about half of them would need the attention of a local physician.

It should be noted that we cannot without further study assume that an explanation fitting the occurrence of deaths by accidents will also fit the minor injuries (cf. Iskrant & Joliet 1968, p. 15).

Information collected by Iversen (1974) suggested that material loss du to accidents happens with a frequency somewhere between 2,500 times and 5,000 times higher than fatal work accidents.

The highly skewed distribution of accidents is notable. Between 50 and 80% of all accidents are accounted for by 5—10% of all persons involved in accidents. There seems to be something that can be called accident proneness, which manifests itself much more in some than in others (cf. Enig 1954).

So far, however, it has not been possible to identify personal characteristics as relevant to accidents other than those discussed in section 3 and those discussed in the present section, i.e. sex, age, diseases and impairment, fatigue, and alcohol customs.

4.3. Transport Risk

It is normal in tables on mortality to compute the risk of dying for constant unit of time and for constant unit of population. The unit of time will usually be the year and the unit of population will most commonly be 10^3, 10^5, or 10^6 persons depending upon the frequency of the cause of death studied.

However, for various purposes it may be convenient to operate with a smaller unit of time than a year, because one may be concerned with risky events that not only differ in lethality per time unit of exposure but also differ in regard to duration of exposure that people normally experience.

Since the normal year contains close to 9,000 hours and since these hours will be distributed with at most 2,000 for work and 1,000 for transport, it will be seen that about 6,000 hours are left for home and recreation. The expected distribution of 94,000 accidental deaths, as in USA 1956, should be the following, with assumed equal risk per hour.

	Expected	Observed	$\dfrac{O}{E}$
Transport 1/9	10,444	45,000	4.31
Work 2/9	20,889	14,000	.67
Home and Recr. 6/9	62,667	35,000	.56
	94,000	94,000	

The time spent on transport is more than 4 times more risky than expected under the condition of equal hourly risk. Work appears to be only slightly more risky than home and recreation. In fact the home and recreation time may be divided into two approximately equal parts: hours awake and hours asleep. Let us assume that no fatal accidents occur during sleep, which is probably close to the truth. it then follows that the time awake receives an observed over expected score of 1.12 and is thus much more risky than the time at work. The major explanation for this relationship is that the working population is biologically better fitted for survival than the home population. In particular, the part of the population aged 70 or more is absent in most work places and it is this age category that is most exposed to fatal home accidents.

The abnormally high risk per hour of exposure involved in transport was verified by Chesnais (1976, p. 254) for France. Fatal accidents during the journey to and from work constitute more than 40% of about 4000 annual workplace-connected accidental deaths in France. Studies have shown that workers have on the average 1 hour's journey for 8 hours work. Per million workers 300 were killed in 1963, 170 at the place of work, 130 during transport to and from work. The figure 130 should be multiplied by 8, giving 1040 deaths per million workers killed during transport with the same exposure as for work proper. The journey to work is thus seen to be 6 times as dangerous as work itself.

Sowby (1965) computed a measure of risk of dying per occupant hour as follows:

Total vehicle mileage x mean number of occupants per vehicle divided by speed per hour = occupant hours of exposure = TP.
Next compute
$D(TP)^{-1} \times 10^9$ = Md = a measure of deadliness where D = number of deaths.
Thus Sowby found that Md was distributed as follows by vehicle in England 1960:
motor cycle 6600
motor scooter 3100
moped 2600
pedal cycle 960
private car 570
railway 50
public service vehicle 30

Of course the estimates needed for arriving at values of TP may deviate from true values, but the extreme differences are likely to be valid.

These transport vehicle estimates could be compared with similarly calculated data by B. Lundberg giving the risk per 10^9 hours of occupant exposure for high quality international air transport as 2400, for private cars in the USA as 950, and for railroad and buses also in the USA as 80.

In particular, both studies agree that the private car exceeds the railroad and buses in riskiness at least by a factor of 10.

In France 16,545 persons were killed in 1972 while travelling by motorcar but only 452 among those who travelled by train, boat, or airplane (Chesnais 1976, Table 47 p. 142)[3]

Arner (1970), who studied fatal accidents among seamen, found that at least 56% of accidental deaths occurred while the ship was in harbor.

This happened in spite of the fact that many more hours are spent at sea than in harbor. Again the high risk of land transport is stressed. In addition, the seaman in foreign ports is frequently subject to severe handicaps because of ignorance of foreign language and culture, because of alcoholism, and simple inability to swim.

Starr (1969) discovered that the logarithm of two measures of mining risk seemed to be positive linear functions of the hourly wage. It suggested that people in general might be more willing to take risks in activities the more they benefited from such activities. The railroad is not so risky as the automobile, but people will still prefer the automobile if they benefit more from transport by automobiles than from transport by railroad or even if they only believe that they do so.

The risk of motor-vehicle transport was calculated by assuming 1.5 persons per car and 400 hours per year as average car use. Since the number of cars in the USA in 1969 was about 80 millions and the number of car accidental deaths about 50,000 per year, we find with the author that this activity has a per capita per hour risk of one chance in a million.

The annual benefit from the car was assumed to be what it costs to operate per person + the value of time saved per person.

Railroad travel can be similarly assessed as to risk and benefit. Starr calculates a per capita and exposure hour risk between 10^{-7} and 10^{-8} and hence a many times more safe transport than by automobile. The annual benefit from railroad transport is what the railroads charge the average customer in the course of a year. This annual benefit estimate is about 10^{-3} of the automobile benefit per year.

The average hourly per capita risk of dying is of course for an industrial society approximately $10^{-2} \times 10^{-4} = 10^{-6}$.

Road traffic accounted for 30% of male accidental deaths in France 1951—55. The corresponding figure for females was 16%. By 1967 this percentage has increased to 44 for males and 24 for females. In 1972 the figure for both sexes combined was 49 (Chesnais 1976). Vallin & Chesnais (1975), working with recently corrected figures for traffic mortality, showed that in the same year 1972 the death toll per million from traffic accidents alone was 380 for both sexes combined, being 541 for males and 188 for females.

Bö (1972) in a study of road accidents in Oslo and environment in 1968 listed three possible causes of accidents: road, road-user and vehicle. He observed that the road-user was involved in 76% of all causes mentioned, while the vehicle was only mentioned in 2% of all causes mentioned. The average number of causes mentioned per accident by those who filled in Bö's questionnaire was 1.5. Altogether 1757 accidents were analyzed. A rather commom driving error could be labeled inappropriate speed, i.e. too high considering the quality of the road, the density of traffic, etc., or compared to the attentiveness of the driver.[4] Another main driving error was failure to conform to the rules of the road (driving on the wrong side of the road, not giving way to traffic from the right). Alcohol to the extent of heavy intoxication (1 g/l or more alcohol in the blood) was involved in 7% of the accidents. Rumpf et al. (1976, Vol. 2, p. 104) estimated that 70—76% of all causes of (German) car accidents were connected with the driver.

The dominant role of the road-user in accident causation may in the case of car drivers be explained by the multiple determination of accident-free driving. Shaw & Sichel (1971) stressed that «it is usually necessary that he (the driver) meets certain basic minimum standards on a number of equally important factors such as ability, health and vision».

It must be considered well established that a main fatal accident determinant is the average daily traffic of a road section. And hence in general the number of fatal accidents on roads per year per capita depends in most nations on the relative number of cars (cf. Svalastoga 1970 and sources cited there).

In the 1960s this dependence on the traffic load was universal in the Western World, except for United States' experience after the 1930s.

The author interpreted the American deviation as due to higher automotive adaptation with higher car density (cf. also Ceder & Livneh 1978).

Svenson (1978, p. 267) expressed himself rather emphatically on the determinants of road traffic risk: «if everyone could drive slowly, alert, and alone on a road with clear visibility, traffic risks would be very small».

Svenson addressed himself to the psychological characteristics of drivers and noted that it has not been possible to generalize on the characteristics of high-risk drivers. Norman (1962) pointed out that a simple random distribution of accidents would produce a small percent of persons with multiple accidents. Young drivers (ages below 25) were consistently more risky drivers than others according to Svenson.

He noted (p. 270) that a large amount of experimental evidence has documented that man tends to be too optimistic and overconfident in his decisions. He continued: «In many situation this may be a virtue, but in the context of road traffic the value of this human «trait» is probably negative».

He furthermore noted a main advantage of the private care: it is «almost always» faster than public transportation over short or medium distances. Surprisingly this even held for Stockholm rush hour traffic.

According to Accident Facts 1968, here cited from Roberts (1971) motor-vehicle deaths killed 1,650,000 persons in the USA from 1900 through to 1967 or an annual loss of 25,000 lives. In comparison Roberts with the same source listed American war deaths in all wars 1775—1967 as follows:[5]

Revolutionary War (1775—1783)	4,435
War of 1812 (1812—1815)	2,260
Mexican War (1846—1848)	13,283
Civil War (1861—1865)	
Union Forces	364,511
Confederate Forces	133,821
Spanish-American War (1898)	2,446
World War I (1917—1918)	116,708
World War II (1941—1945)	407,316
Korean War (1950—1953)	54,246
Viet Nam War (1961—1967)	19,213

It will be seen that war deaths 1775—1967 add up to 1,118,239 or considerable less than the road-accident toll for a much smaller time period.

4.4 Home Risk

Backett (1967) used American and English mortality statistics ca. 1960 to document that mortality from domestic accidents is very modest in the age interval 5—64 for both sexes, that the age interval 0—4 and particularly 0—1 is many times more risky, but that the greatest risk of death from domestic accidents only occurs after age 64. Whereas the differences between the sexes were small and insignificant for persons under 65 years of age, females were under greater risk than males in the age category 65 years of age or more. Falls constituted a main cause of fatal accidents and between 50% and 80% of all falls in a sample of Western nations investigated by Backett about 1960 proved to be domestic falls (cf. also Thygerson 1977, p. 173).

In a sample of American and European nations falls were around 1960 the dominant type of domestic accident leading to death. The major competitors among lethal domestic accidents were fire (Canada and USA), or poisoning (e.g. United Kingdom).

Waller (1978) reported from a study of elderly people in Vermont, USA, that 40% of a sample of injured persons had experienced at least one fall during the previous 12 months, and even his comparison sample reported that 32% had experienced falls during the same time period.

Among more than 3200 deaths due to domestic falls in England and Wales in 1962, persons ages 65 years and more accounted for 89%. About 2 out of 3 of these were females.

A study of MacQueen, cited by Backett, noticed that the risk of falls tended to increase with the number of flights of stairs to be climbed (ibid p. 81). A curvilinear relationship between domestic accident mortality and social status was documented for England and Wales 1949—53. Mortality among males and married females aged 20—64 years was somewhat higher both towards the bottom and, in particular, towards the top of the social hierarchy.

Ammundsen & Jesperson (1953) had already noted the higher risks at the lower end of the status ladder. From observations in Copenhagen 1952 they noted that accidents with toys could frequently be ascribed to the poor quality of the toys used. Accidents in connection with house-cleaning and splinters from the floor and kitchen-table were ascribed to insufficient upkeep of furniture and tools. The authors suggested that many accidents were caused by too much furniture and a high population-density chiefly among occupiers of small apartments.

Jensenius analyzed the spatial distribution of accidents and found that accidents in the home were most likely to occur in the living-room (about 40%). Four other places in or around the house had each 10—15% of all home accidents: stairs, yard, garden, kitchen.

Pedersen (1967) noted the elaborate system built up in Denmark to combat accidents on the road and at work, whereas accidents in the home had received very little attention. He collected data on 1772 patients residing in or around the city of Randers, Denmark, and treated for accidents that had taken place inside the four walls of the home, a stricter definition of home than the one customarily used.

Of particular interest is the distribution of accidents by room, which ranks the most accident-visited rooms as follows:

Room	Number of accidents
Living-room	619
Kitchen	537
Stairs	228
Hobbyroom	135
Bedroom	90

These counts would be still more meaningful if related to the product PT defined above: persons times average time exposure in given location. Even without a precise knowledge of PT it is clear that stairs must have a rather modest PT value.

If PT is measured in person — minutes per day the kitchen might well obtain a PT value of 100 or more. In contrast, the stairs would have to be used quite a lot and by many people to give even a PT value of 10. If these assumptions are realistic, then it follows that the stairs are one of the most dangerous places in a home and markedly more dangerous than the kitchen.

Lossing & Goyette (1957) analyzed 1000 non-fatal home accidents treated at hospitals in the Ottawa region of Canada. Home was defined as dwelling place + premises like yard, garage, etc. Falls constituted the dominant accident and stairs appeared as a major injurious agent.

About 60% of the victims were young people below 17 years of age, and only 3 percent were aged 70 or more. In contrast, the fatal accidents in Canada in 1954, which numbered 2128 persons, included 36% who were 70 years old or older. Children under five years of age constituted 39% in the non-fatal sample and 32% among the victims of fatal accidents.

The authors concluded that three-quarters of all the accidents studied could have been prevented by no more than a reasonable amount of care and forethought.

4.5 Work Risk

One of the most important empirical generalizations in regard to industrial accidents was reported by Koshal & Koshal (1974).

They found that the accident rate per 10^3 workers could be predicted from a knowledge of four factors, of which two tended to reduce the accident rate («average monthly earnings» and «percent female employees»), and two tended to increase the accident rate («overtime hours as percent of total hours worked», and «number of employees per plant»). Rather similar results were obtained from comparable studies conducted in the USA, in India, in Japan, and in Hungary.

Arner (1970) investigated 1027 fatal accidents in the Norwegian merchant marine occurring during the years 1957—64. This number was believed to represent a nearly total enumeration of persons accidentally killed during the period.

Seamen were considered a Norwegian high risk group. Average accident mortality for males 15—69 years of age is given by Arner as 770 deaths per million per year in the time interval 1957—64. The corresponding figure for Norwegian seamen in foreign waters was 2760 or 3.6 times higher.

Alcohol consumption could be approximately ascertained for about 350 of the total sample. Among these about 88% were characterized as intoxicated and 20% were heavily intoxicated. Only 2% were labeled sober, while 10% were characterized as sick. (Arner 1970, p. 120 Table 47).

In general Norwegian seamen appear from statistics as more then the average handicapped by an increased risk not only of alcoholism but also of crime and mental disease.

Otterland (1960) classified 1775 Swedish merchant seafarers who died 1945—54 according to cause of death.

Table 4.1 Accidental death among Norwegian seamen by cause (Arner 1970).

Causes
1) *Sudden or extreme environmental change:*   %
   Shipwreck   11
   Explosion, fire   7

2) *Individual deviation:*
   Drowning*   33
   Falling   13
   Poisoning   8
   Land-traffic victim   4
   Suicide   15
   Homicide   3

3) N.A.   6

    100
N = 1027

* Including 5% who were found floating in the water.

Medical causes accounted for 803 cases or 45.24% of the sample, while «accidents and violence» accounted for 971 cases or 54.70%. One case could not be classified. «Accidents and Violence» were distributed as follows: (Table 21 p. 74).

Accidents	714[6]
Suicide	236
Homicide	21
	971

The great majority died while the ship was in port, only a few while it was at sea. Among the 803 seamen with a medical cause of death no fewer than 599 died in hospital or at home. Although most suicides took place on board the ship, accidents were likely to happen elsewhere. The after-effect of the harbor visit was observed in a heightened mortality during the 12 hours after leaving the harbor:

Site of death	Accidents, Homicides	Suicide
On board	281	138
In hospital ashore	50	10
In home or hotel	14	53
On land, leisure	90	22
On way to or from ship	183	11
Other locations	117	2

Otterland documented that the median age of seamen dying from accidents ranged from 28.5 per year for «fall-drowning» to 32.2 for «accidents to ship»; for suicide cases the median age was 34.4 and for homicide cases 28.8. His mixed category «homicide or suicide or accident» showed a mean age of 34.2 and thus resembled most the suicide cases in regard to age. The seamen are also shown to die at an earlier age for any given cause. The total group showed a surplus mortality compared to average Swedish male mortality by age in the same chronological peirod. While 1775 seamen died, only 828 were expected to die in the average Swedish male population of age 15 to 69. The total result may also be expressed as follows:

$$Y = 2.14x$$

where y = number of seamen dying
and x = number of Swedish males aged 15—69 expected to die.

This surplus mortality was most visible for the category accidents + homicide, where the ratio $\frac{y}{x}$ increased to 7.14. Suicides had a ratio $\frac{y}{x} = 4.37$. Ottinger found 18% cases of alcoholism[7] in his total material, but among the suicides more than 50% of the cases mentioned excessive drinking (p. 233).

4.6 Recreational Risk

Some recreations are more risky than others. Some of the more risky ones among them were analyzed by Sowby (1965) and given the estimated number dying per hour of exposure in a 1000 million population:

Canoeing	10,000
Mountaineering	27,000
Motorcycle racing	35,000
Rock climbing	40,000
Professional boxing	70,000
Flat racing	100,000
Jockey racing	500,000

4.7 Sex and Age

Chesnais (1976) showed that the $\frac{male}{female}$ ratio of accident rates between between 1856 and 1925 had a very limited range from 4.2 to 5.5. Male victims thus tended to be about five times as numerous as female victims. After 1925 the ratio has tended to decline, so that as of 1966—70 males were still in the majority among accidental deaths, but the ratio had dropped from 3.4 (1926—30) to 1.6 (1966—70). For the period after 1925 Chesnais could use the more reliable cause of death statistics published since 1906, whereas for the earlier period he had to use legal statistics (*La statistique judiciaire* going back to 1825).

Chesnais presented a breakdown by sex and age for the years 1968—70. Age and sex specific rates are given for each five-year interval from age 5 to age 59. For the years 0—4 a separate breakdown for the first year of life and the following four is given. From age 60 to age 79 only decennial figures were presented, and persons aged 80 years or older were treated as one category. It held for males and for females that the least dangerous, and hence best protected, years were the years from age 5 to age 14. The early years of life proved to be somewhat more exposed. This held specifically for the first year of life, which was more dangerous than any five-year interval before age 20 for males and before age 70 for females.

Although the rates for males increased by a factor of four from age interval 5—14 to age interval 15—29, this average was only slightly lower for the years 30—44, and from age 55 on the male starts on the most risky path of his career, the path becoming more risky with increasing age. At age 80 and above the risk per year of dying by accident, although only about one in two thousand, was still 29 times higher than the 5—14 age interval male risk. The female sex appears consistently as the better protected sex at all ages below 80. The female superiority appears particularly pronouced in the age intervals from 25 to 49 where the female accident rates are less than $\frac{1}{4}$ of the male rates.

A similar table for the years 1931—33 again revealed the superprotection of the ages 5—14 for both sexes as well as the higher risk of the first five years of life. Also verified was the increasing risk by age, but in this table the rather regular increase started already at age 15. Females appear as even better protected than in 1968—70. The female rates were less than or equal to one-fifth of the male rates from age 20 to age 55.

The male sex was still the most accident-prone sex at all ages below 75 years in all major Western European nations as well as in the USA and Sweden in the period 1950—74 or 1960—74. In most of these countries the genralization also held for the age-class 75—79. In some instances the critical value was 85 years, and in the USA as of 1970—74 the males were dominant at all ages.

The total difference in accident rate was not very extreme in the Western World as of 1970—74. In none of the nations USA, France, West Germany, Italy, England, Sweden did the quotient $\frac{male\ rate}{female\ rate}$ leave the interval 1.3—2.4. However, a quite different picture develops if age is held constant.

The American data for 1970—74 showed that the male rate is less than twice the female rate in childhood and after age 75. Between age 15 and age 49 the quotient ranged between 3.0 and 4,6 (for the years 20—24) and between age 50 and age 74 the range is from 2.0 to 2.8 (World Health Statistics Annual 1978).

World Health's analysis of accidents for the quinquennium 1970—74 documented a persistent correlation between accident rate and age in England, France, and the USA. This correlation is not linear. there is not one but three accident peaks: age 0—5, age 15—25, and age 80—84. From age 40 to age 84 the accident rate is increasing in all three nations as well as in Sweden. Sweden deviates by having only the two last mentioned of the three peaks.

In the USA the proportion of deaths due to accidents in the age group 1—34 years and particularly in the subgroup 15—24 years had been increasing in the time interval 1900—60 and most strongly between 1935 and 1955.

This happened while at the same time accidents per capita went down or remained steady in the same time interval. The reason for the increased importance as cause of death was that other killers more rapidly came under medical control. thus in the age group 15—24 around 1900 accidents was only one of five leading causes of death. The others were tuberculosis, typfoid fever, influenza & pneumonia, and diseases of the heart. By 1960 all these causes except accidents had been reduced by a factor of $\frac{1}{10}$ or more (Iskrant & Foliet, 1968, pp. 3,4).

Dreyer & Nørregaard (1957) found a regular decline in the risk of accidental death among children of both sexes as their age increased from 0 to 14 years. Boys started life with a fatal accident risk per million population of 772 during their first year of life. As they reached the age interval 12 ± 2 years they were down to 174. Girls declined from 559 to 51. The higher male risk was observed in all of five subcategories by age, but increased from $\frac{male\ rate}{female\ rate} = 1.38$ during the first year of life to at ratio of 3.14 for the age interval 12 ± 2. The authors investigated all accidental deaths during the first 15 years of life in Denmark 1931—55. A total number of 6844 such deaths occurred. The above figures refer to the deaths occurring 1951—55 only, but figures for the other years investigated confirmed the trends here documented.

Accidental deaths accounted for 4% of Danish male deaths in the age category 0—14 in the period 1931—35 but increased to 12% in 1951—55. Corresponding figures for females were respectively 3 and 8. According to Drejer & Nørregaard, children with vision — or hearing — defects are over-represented both among accidents generally and among lethal accidents. In the present text the major emphasis is on social factors. However, it is well known that bodily defects or imbalances can increase the risk of accidents. Thygerson (1977 pp. 50—56) listed fatigue, diabetes, epilepsy, and heart disease as particularly accident-prone conditions.

5. Suicide

De Videnskabsmænd, der hidintil have gjort den menneskelige Aands Virksomhed til Gjenstand for deres Forskninger, have næsten udelukkende valgt den speculative Vej. Uden her at ville indlade mig paa nogen Vurdering af de saaledes vundne Resultater, kan jeg ikke tilbageholde det Spørgsmaal, om denne Vej skulde være den eneste, ad hvilken man kunde erholde Kundskab om Menneskets aandelige Liv, eller om maaske ikke en ganske modsat, den naturvidenskabelige, skulde kunne afgive nye og interessante Bidrag.

C. J. Kayser
Om Selvmord i Kongeriget Danmark.
København, 1846.

Selvmord og dødshjelp er et nederlag for samfunnet. Det er et nederlag fordi det er vår oppgave å gjøre tilværelsen slik at det er bedre å leve enn å være død. Om noen foretrekker å dø, viser det at vi ikke har lykkes.

H. Ofstad
Dagbladet (Norwegian newspaper).
Kronikk 8 July 1978.

5.1 Trend

In few areas of research has so much disagreement appeared even among modern researchers as in regard to suicide trend. Is suicide becoming more common or less with increasing industrialization or is there a steady state rate only weakly influenced if at all by industrialization? There are at least three possible and different answers to this question:

1) increase
2) steady state
3) decrease

All three views are represented among researchers who have published their views after World War II. The theory of an increasing tendency towards suicide «in the civilized states of Europe and America» was proposed already by Morselli (1882, p. 29), and was based on the suicide statistics available which with but one exception showed an increasing trend.

At the First Criminological Congress convened in Rome 1885, Morselli expressed himself rather sweepingly as follows:
«le nombre des suicides augmente, celui des homicides diminue avec l'instruction», and he concluded:
«Suicide et homicide sont deux phenomè de la lutte pour l'existence. Leur consequence est la même: l'élimination du faible» (Morselli (1886—87).
Ferri (1895) was likewise convinced of the upward trend of suicide in the Western World, and Verkko, the foremost violence researcher in Scandinavia, likewise concluded that for a sufficiently long observational period the trend of suicide is increasing, the trend of homicide decreasing (op.cit. p. 162).

Adherents to the growth theory could point to a large collection of statistical data which rather invariantly recorded growing suicide rates with the advance of time.

Halbwachs (1930) tabulated quinquennial rates of suicide for 11 European nations. He averaged these eleven rates and obtained a series growing with only a few and minor setbacks from 91 suicides per million 1836—1845 to 175 for 1922—1925. Inspection of his statistics for each of the nations reveals that most of these nations show a rather close approximation to the average trend.

Finland, with the longest series of suicide statistics existing, provided a rather strong support for the theory of an increasing trend. Sweden with a series starting only 20 years later provided another strong support for the increasing trend assumption.

In direct opposition to the traditional view of a suicide-modernization syndrome, Chesnais (1976) seemed to posit the theory that the advance of industrial civilization entails a reduction in the suicide rate.

He noted a confirmation for this theory in France and for a group of industrialized nations where suicide data could be compared over a 40-year period (1927—29 to 1966—67) (Chesnais 1976, p. 100).

Kruijt (1977) was not willing to assume that suicide in the twentieth-century Western World followed an invariant growth model. On the bases of his own studies he concluded that during the period c. 1900 — c. 1940 the centrally situated countries of Western Europe and the Anglo-Saxon cultural sphere USA, Canada, Australia, and New Zealand showed a stabilization or decline in the suicide rate: only in Northern and Southern Europe was the rate increasing. Kruijt explained the latter deviation as due to a lag in the industrialization process in the countries concerned.

For the period after World War II Kruijt found an increasing suicide rate in central European nations for both sexes, excepting only English males.

The cause guessed at by Kruijt was an increase of anomia in the midst of the prosperous 1960s.

A good representative for the steady state theory of suicide, i.e. the theory that suicide has been as common in the past as in the present, is the British researcher Hair.

Hair (1971) found reason to suspect that the statistics of suicides did not include more than a part of all suicides. Although the figures for suicide available for England or parts of England c. 1640 — c. 1860 tend to be lower than the 1970 value, Hair was still most inclined to favor a steady state theory.

Dublin (1963) considered that the rates of suicide around 1960 in the USA would come closer to the truth if they were multiplied by a factor in the neighborhood of 1.3.

Douglas (1967) presented a carefully reasoned exposition in which he rejected the theory of a nineteenth-century true increase in suicidal behavior and presented several reasons why the statistics of suicide for the early part of the nineteenth-century and earlier should be distrusted.

Suicide in the Western World at many times and places has been or is (cf. also Douglas, 1967 chapter 12):

1) a religious sin
2) a sociological stigmatization of the suicide's family
3) an extra economic loss through insurance forfeiture
4) hard to distinguish from accidental death
5) imperfectly registered

It follows that statistics of suicide are difficult to interpret in relation to time. Variations over time may be due to variations in one or more of the factors mentioned rather than to real changes in suicidal frequency.[1]

Halbwachs' series of increasing suicide rates, recorded 1836—1925, need not reflect an increasing tendency to commit suicide.

The period 1836—1925 was at the same time characterized by an increasing European efficiency in the registration of the causes of death. There was also a strong movement towards a secularization in beliefs and customs making concealment of suicide less important. These two factors may in fact well be sufficient to explain the upward movement of the nineteenth-century European suicide rates.

From the tabulated material presented here, it may be seen that even in the twentieth-century, with its more trustworthy statistics in advanced industrial nations, the three theories mentioned may each of them be illustrated in at least one nation.

Thus Swedish suicide statistics not only document the commonly seen nineteenth-century increase, but they continue increasing throughout the first three-quarters of the twentieth-century. On the other hand, both USA and France show a marked decline in the course of this century. The steady state theorists can point to England and to Japan for statistical support.

In fact the English records for the twentieth century come rather close to the sinusoidal function (Allen 1959, p. 116 seq.).

$$Y = A \cos(\omega t + \in)$$
in which A = amplitude measured from the average level and with period $\dfrac{2\pi}{\omega}$ and phase characterized by maximum value of y for $\omega t + \in = 0$
Using the following value for the constants
$$A = 17$$
$$\omega = \frac{1}{4}$$
$$\in = -\pi$$

one obtains the theoretical curve drawn in Fig. 5.1a.

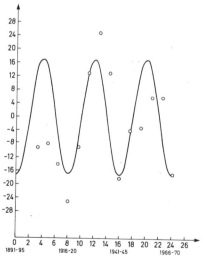

Fig. 5.1a England and Wales 1901 – 1960 (suicides per million population) minus 110. Observed rates (0) compared with a cyclic model. Cp. Table 3.1.

Note to Fig. 5.1a:
  $y = S\ P^{-1}\ 10^6 - 110$
  S = suicides
  P = population
  X = Time in units of $7 = 3{,}1416$ years, $0 : 1891 - 1895$
  O = empirical data from table 3.1
  Observed data compared with theoretical curve

  $$Y = 17 \cos \left(\frac{t}{4} - \pi \right)$$

For a cyclic theory to hold good a social system would have to be subject to a time-regulated increase and decrease in the total resultant of forces conducive to suicide. Since such a clock-like mechanism seems rather unlikely in a changing world, it would probably take a much more complex theory to describe the course actually followed by suicidal deaths relative to population.

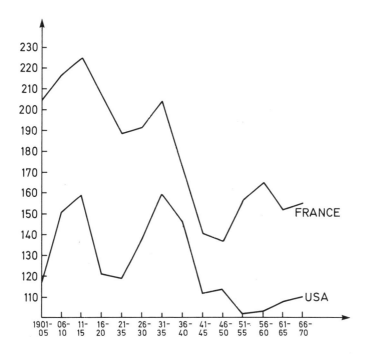

Fig. 5.1b France $1901 - 1970$ (upper curve), USA $1901 - 1970$ (lower curve). Suicides per million population. Cp. Tables 3.2 and 3.3.

In 1954 Henry and Short had already formulated a cyclical theory of American suicide: suicide rises in depression and falls in prosperity.

In Japan suicide over the last 100 years has tended to swing back and forth between 100 and 300 suicides per million population per year. For the period 1868—1926, Igo (1978) found an everage of 190 suicides per million per year. Kato (1969) noted that the Western World has only about 1/3 female suicides in contrast to an oriental ratio closer to 2/3.

The author is inclined to favor the steady state theory for the short and perhaps middle run, but in the long run the possibility cannot be negated that societies through more efficient social engineering may learn to alleviate social isolation and to strengthen individual capacity for social living. Then suicide would gradually become more rare.

The steady state theory will have to allow for fluctuations, perhaps mostly random, but in addition conditioned by variations in activity of economic or military nature.

5.2 Epidemiology

Studies of suicide in the Western World have regularly shown that certain individual characteristics and certain social system characteristics are rather invariably related to suicide. Among individual characteristics the most important seem to be sex, age, and familial status. The optimal combination is female sex, youthful age, married, and having children. The super risky combination is male sex, old age, divorced or single, or widowed, no children (cf. Stengel 1965, Pærregaard 1963, Rettserstöl 1970).

Chesnais' tables show that suicide in France since 1826 has been consistently more frequent among males than among females. The male rates per million population are rather consistently three times or more above the female rates throughout the period 1826—1970.

Hartelius (1957) noted an increase in female suicide rate in Sweden from the 1925—37 period to the 1938—50 period, which he interpreted as a product of increasing emancipation, secularization and urbanization.

In Denmark the suicide rate of males c. 1800 — c. 1960 changed from 3—4 times that of females to only 2 times the female rate (Pærregaard 1963). In Norway the increasing rate by age was tabulated by Retterstöl (1970, p. 257). The figures for males in 1966 increased from 66 to 221 per million with age increasing from 15—29 to 50—59. The figures remained high up to age 80 and then a strong decrease took place. Female suicides increased from 16 to 79 with age increasing from 15—29 to 40—49. Thereupon figures remained high until age 70 when a strong decrease took place.

Rudfeld (1962) analyzed suicidal deaths in Denmark in 1956, going back to the original death certificates. She found that 29% of 995 observed cases had at some time in their life been defined as mentally ill, and treated medically for this disease. On the basis of previous research in Denmark the risk of becoming mentally ill sometime during one's lifetime is .12. Since the suicide cases had, on the average, only lived through 5/7 of their expected life, it follows that the risk of belonging to the group of mentally ill is .09. If suicides were a random sample of the population, we should expect only 9% mentally ill in the sample. It is natural to explain the strong deviation observed as due to a higher than average tendency towards suicide among mentally ill persons. Laerum et al. (1979) estimated that mentally ill persons, defined as persons with earlier psychiatric hospitalization, had much higher suicide risks than «normal» persons, marital status and sex constant. Thus «normal» persons of male sex and married were estimated to have 23 suicides per 100,000, but if they had been in a psychiatric hospital, the suicide risk was estimated as 5—6 times greater, depending upon psychiatric diagnosis. The step-up of the suicide risk was 11 times for married femeals who had attended a psychiatric hospital.

Physical illness was present in 25% of Rudfeld's Danish sample and severe illness characterized 9%. the best explanation seemed to be, as for mental illness, that the physically ill and particularly serious cases have a higher than average suicide risk.

A WHO Chronicle editorial 1975 (Vol. 29:193—198) stressed the similarity of suicide, drug-dependence, alcoholism, and accident-prone road traffic, all being more or less self-destructive; mental illness might perhaps be added. It was maintained that among young people aged 15—24 years neither drug-dependence nor alcoholism are important suicide causes. the important causes were said to be mental illness, and such environmental causes as family breakdown, urbanization, and social change in general. Suicidal contagion was seen as a real risk.

Barrett & Franke (1970) made an international study of five causes of death termed psychogenic: suicide, homicide, ulcer, cirrhosis, and hypertension. The only stable cross-nation correlation among these causes was the one between suicide and ulcer ($r = .4 - .5$).

Pai (1976) reported on violent deaths in Bombay 1942—61. The total toll of violent deaths relative to population was 620 per million population in 1962 and thus rather similar to the incidence in USA and Japan. The most deviant trait of Bombay violent deaths was the remarkable low level of suicides (1962:5 per million population). The author ascribed this protection against suicide to the «fatalistic philosophy of Indians», which he hypothesized as an effective buffer against failure.

Two social system states are regularly related to suicide: economic crisis and war.

A nation tends to experience an increase in its suicide rate in times of economic crisis or decline. In contrast wars tend to depress the suicide rate.

These invariances have long been noted and were recently confirmed for most nations participating in World War II.

It will be noted that these invariances may be explained by Durkheim's theory (cf. sec. 5.3), but Pærregaard (1963) noted that the relationship between suicide and war had also been explained by some researchers as due to reduced alcohol consumption in wartime or to war-conditioned decrease in registration standard (cf. also Dublin 1963, on the USA, and Kato 1969, on Japan.

Ogburn & Thomas (1922) reported a correlation of − .74 between suicide rate in one hundred US cities 1900—1920 and an index of business conditions.

Halbwachs (1930) documented for several nations in Europe the relationship (existing c. 1830 — c. 1930 between suicide and urbanization. This documentation may be said to support two generalization:

1) With increasing urbanization (either more cities or larger cities or both) increasing suicide.[2]
2) Since with increasing urbanization even the countryside will be penetrated by urban civilization, the difference between suicide rates between cities by size and between cities and rural regions, declines.

Suicide tends to be more frequent in Protestant than in Catholic or Jewish regions or areas.

Dublin (1963) stressed that the Catholic faith and the Jewish faith, to a much greater degree that the Protestant faith, are not only religions but are also systems of social organization.

Henry & Short (1954) concentrated their work around the explanation of suicide and homicide in the United States. They regarded frustration as the main cause of aggression both suicidal and homicidal. Frustration was seen as a product of economic fluctuations.

But whether these frustrations resulted in suicides or homicides depended upon the integration and control of individual behavior within social systems (cf. Durkheim 1897). Where this integration and control was weak, suicide was predicted. Whereas the latter prediction could be verified, the homicidal prediction was judged as only tentatively confirmed by the data (pp. 77, 96).

Pærregaard (1963) pointed out in her comprehensive review of suicide literature that suicide is considered contagious according to a rather commonly accepted view, although no formal testing of this theory exists.

According to Retterstöl (1970), suicide attempts tend to be 7—8 times as frequent as suicides.

5.3 Theory

The attempts to explain suicide has so far led to two major sociological traditions: the European Durkheimian tradition and the American ecological tradition (cf. Douglas 1967). The geographical labels refer to the original location of the traditions or schools.

At present durkheimians and ecologists concerned with suicide can probably be found whereever scientific sociology can diffuse without meeting ideological barriers to knowledge.

Sociological theories of suicide attempt to identify variables in the social system that may be related to the occurrence of suicide. It seems well documented that in addition to social system characteristics, individual characacteristics are relevent to the more complete explanation of suicide. The delimitation of areas of individual vulnerability (in particular mental disease and alcoholism) may be important to suicide prevention.

The ecological approach to suicide has the advantage of taking into account both conditions in society and individual characacteristics.

Ellsworth Faris wrote in his introduction to Cavan's study of Suicide in Chicago (1928) that individual persons commit suicide, but Cavan's study documented that suicide is not wholly an individual phenomenon. There was in the social environment of suicides in Chicago rather consistent evidence of social malfunctioning or disorganization. Cavan's description of the top suicidal districts, which around 1920 were located in or close to the city center was frequently colorful and rich with empirical observations of the neighborhoods concerned. These were typically regions dominated by cheap lodging houses and pawnshops, and places where divorce and homicide happened often. These neighborhoods were also dominant in regard to frequency of psychoses, deaths from alcoholism, and number of houses of prostitution.

The lodging house population was a population without family life and without neighborhood activities: a shifting population of unattached men and women.

Cavan documented for the city of Chicago a strong variation across the city from 870 suicides per million per year in the Loop c. 1920 to only 10 in the South Shore. In the Loop 78% of population was male.

Another classic study in the ecological tradition is due to Calvin Schmid, who in 1928 published a study of suicide in Seattle 1914—1925. In this study Schmid is mostly concerned with social system characteristics: neighborhood, population processes in particular migration, social disorganization, anomymity and economic factors. But in addition he stressed individual factors. In his tabulation of diagnoses for 747 out of a total of 901 suicides, social disorders account directly for only 40% of the cases. The remaining 60% are assumed to have become suicide victims primarily, at least, from personal weaknessess; about 28% are said to suffer from mental or nervous disorders, including alcoholism and drug addiction, and 32% suffered from various physical ailments. The same stress on both social and individual causes, although with main emphasis on social causes, is found in Faris (1955), where high suicide rates are said to be produced by the convergence of three factors: social isolation, personal crisis, and a personality factor.

Schmid & Arsdol (1955) likewise stressed both sociological conditions (differential incidence by intra-urban location, by marital status and by occupation) and at least individual factors such as sex and age. Verkko (1951) came very close to the ecological approach.,

Verkko (1951) distinguished between endogenous and exogenous causes of suicide. The endogenous causes are independent of the environment and account for a proportion of suicide which is assumed to be approximately invariant over time and space.

It follows that exogenous, i.e. environmental causes will have to explain most of the variations observed over time and space (p. 119). Endogenous causes appear primarily as psychic disorders (p. 126). Verkko was influenced by J. L. Gillin's successful textbook on social pathology, the third edition of which is cited (Gillin 1946, pp. 157—8). Verkko rejected the more extreme sociological theories of Halbwachs and Dublin-Bunzel. He also rejected the more one-sided psychological theories of Achille-Delmas and of Menninger. Verkko emphasized strongly the importance of alcohol or, as he most frequently expressed it, the «ability to carry liquor». Alcohol was not seen as an exogenous factor but rather as an endogenous factor, an ability tentatively related to Kretschmer's typology of body shapes.

Rudfeld (1962) likewise took the ecological approach; she contended that suicide risk could be expressed as follows:

$$f = F\left(\frac{D}{S}, \frac{dD}{dt}, \frac{dS}{dt}\right)$$

f = suicide risk
F = undefined function of elements in parenthesis
D = personal deviation from average
S = social integration
t = time

This conceptualization, which was developed by Rudfeld assisted by Høgh, seems to be the only formulation of the ecological approach in which variables representing change rates are explicitly suggested.

Durkheim's theory of the social causation of suicide was developed in his 1897 classical monograph on suicide.

According to this theory, suicide (i.e. variations in the suicide rate) depends on the integration of social groups (domestic, territorial or religious) and on the regulation of individuals by social norms.

If integration is weakened by a high development of individualism, suicide is more frequent. If integration is very highly developed, as in some military systems, suicide is also more frequent.

If the social norms break down and individuals are not guided by them, then anomie reigns, and suicide becomes more frequent. If the social norms become too rigid and imperial, then again suicide becomes more frequent (Durkheim 1897, pp. 223—311, cf. Baechler 1975, p. 26).

Although considerable work on operational problems remains to be done in order to put the theory to adequate tests, it is this author's conviction that Durkheim has offered the most promising sociological explanation of suicide.

Durkheim's theory fails to consider the problems posed by the commonness of some of his suicidal states, e.g. anomie due to economic crisis and the relative rarity of actual suicides. The poisoned arrows hit many but kill few. In some sense those who commit suicide must represent a superexposed category with lower than average resistance to suicide.

This seems to be indicated by the over-representation of old males, lower class persons, alcoholics, and persons with behavioral and/or organic diseases.

6. Homicide

6.1 Trend

Homicide rates were investigated for England, France, USA, and Sweden with respect to possible trends, cycles, or steady states.

The general conclusion is that homicide in these nations during the twentieth-century seemed to have found a steady state with very modest seemingly random swings up and down.

Chesnais (1975) surveyed homicide data c. 1950 — c. 1970 on the basis of World Health statistics. To the present author the average figures presented for 1950—54 as against 1969—71 support the view that the temporal variations in the homicide rate in the Northern America — Western Europe area are rather limited and may well be randomly caused. Thus if the median of the two entries is computed, the deviation observed for either 1950—54 or 1969—71 is never as high as one-half the median value.

For some nations the steady state even extended into the nineteenth-century. This was the case in France. In England and Sweden homicide ran considerably higher in the nineteenth-century than in the twentieth. No nineteenth-century American homicide rates have come to the author's attention, but since the nineteenth-century saw the conquest of the major part of the North American continent, it seems highly probable that its homicide rate would reach higher levels than those known for the twentieth-century. The USA experienced a regular and fast decline in homicides by lynching in the period 1890 to 1970. The corresponding rates per capita would show a still speedier decline because of population growth. (See Historical Statistics . . . of the United States).

Henry & Short (1954) fitted second degree equations to homicide data for the USA c. 1920—1940 for whites and non-whites separately and for three different definitions of the American death registration area. Out of 12 coefficients (b or c) relating homicides to time according to the model

$$y = a + bt + ct^2,$$

all but two were negative, and the two exceptions referred to values close to zero. During the period between the world wars American homicides thus tended on the whole to decline, in spite of an initial increase in homicidal frequency (cf. Table 3.3).

Henry & Short (1954, p. 15) furthermore noted a tendency in their data for crimes of violence against persons in general to rise in propserity and to fall during depression.

The French homicide values presented in Chesnais (1976) and here in Table 3.2 are, like the English values, characterized by a very limited variation. For the whole period 1826—1970 the quinquennial averages ranged only between a minimum of 7 homicides per million per year to a maximum of 17 homicides per year, and it is possible to capture all but the two most extreme values in the interval 7 ± 3.

It may be added that the rather likely early nineteenth-century under-registration of cases of operational violence may also apply to homicide in France.

The Swedish homicide rates 1761—1970 ranged between 6 and 22. The very low values towards the beginning of the series should of course be considered with suspicion, but for the most of the nineteenth-century the rates are probably realistic and thus reflect a markedly higher homicide frequency than the twentieth-century data available.

The English series from 1901 to 1975 (Fig. 6.1) is remarkably steady, only ranging between 4 and 9 homicides per million people (based on five years annual averages. All observations are thus inside the span 6 ± 3. According to Hair (1971), the rate of homicide around 1860 in England was about 20 per million.

London homicide rates give higher figures the further back one goes and the same is true for executions. On the basis of such information and general historical information Hair tended to assume that homicide in England had declined over time.

The same may well be true for Scandinavia if a homicide series could be pushed further back in time than the present limit: 1760.

Hanawalt's paper on English homicide in the late Middle Ages seems to give strong support to Hair's assumption of a declining rate of homicide. Hanawalt (1976) noted that the London coroners' rolls listed, on the average, 18 homicides per year for a set of 8 complete annual records within the time interval 1300—1340. The population of London at that time would most likely be 35,000 — 50,000. With a population of 50,000 the annual suicide rate per million becomes 360, an enormously high number by modern standards. Miami had the highest homicide rate of any American city 1948 — 52 with 150 homicides per million. In medieval London or Oxford homicide was more common than accidental death. There were 43 percent more homicides than deaths by accidents in London and 26% more in Oxford.[1] Among the conditions characterizing medieval as against modern England and which might possibly explain the stepped up rate of violence by homicide, Hanawalt pointed to the lower value attributed to human life and to the accepted custom of settling disputes by violence. This custom became strengthened through the expensiveness, slowness, and corruption of legal procedures.

Bouthoul (1970) is clearly also of the opinion that certain types of violence were vastly more common in Europa in the Middle Ages than today. He reminded readers that in the Middle Ages even the smallest cities had their hangman and their gallows (p. 314).

The present author is inclined to accept the theory that homicide declines in frequency as nations become affected by industrialization and urbanization.

Although the empirical basis for this theory is still limited, it nevertheless mut be considered the best hypothesis. As Bouthoul and Hair and others have emphasized and in part documented, the medieval and early modern European environment was a rather harsh environment with an upper class usually armed and a lower class plagued by illness, undernourishment, and ignorance, and all of them more tolerant of violence than are modern Europeans.

6.2 Epidemiology and Theory

World Health statistics from around 1970 analyzed by Chesnais (1975) documented a general tendency towards higher homicide (victim) risk for males than for females. This tendency was still present in Western Europe but was more weakly expressed there than elsewhere.

In Wolfgang's classic study (1958) males predominated both as victims and as offenders.

The offender is according to available experience more likely to be male than a female (Wolfgang 1965, Siciliano 1965, Hansen 1977). In Denmark 1933 — 1970 the ratio was close to 2 to 1 (two male offenders for each female offender).

The most risky male age categories may be said to comprise the years 15—39. The human animal is much more peaceful before and after these critical 25 years.

Victims tend to be somewhat older than offenders (Wolfgang 1958). Siciliano computed the homicide rate per million population by level of urbanization and found a rate of 8 for Copenhagen, 5 for larger cities and 3 for the rest of Denmark. This tendency was also confirmed by Wolfgang and by Hansen.

A frequent observation is that the victims of homicide in 8 or 9 out of 10 cases are either members of the murderer's family or of his group of friends or acquaintances (Svalastoga 1956).

In Hansen's material comprising 756 offenders and 892 victims in Denmark 1946—1970, there were 73% family victims and 21% acquantance victims. Siciliano found 70% family victims. His classification does not yield a figure for acquaintances.

Palmer (1960) developed what he termed an index of physical frustration in order to compare a group of murderers with their brothers. Scores were alloted for birth difficulties, operations, serious illnesses, accidents, and serious beatings.

Murderers had received a much tougher treatment thus measured than had their brothers. The information was, however, collected from the mothers of the murderers and their brothers. The mothers might well have become motivated to remember better the past life of the murderers than that of their brothers.

So far no special theory covering only homicidal behavior seems to exist. All theories that have been pointed to as explanations of homicide have been used to explain also other specific types of violence or violence in general. Among the three theories that Wolfgang (1968) lists as attempts to explain homicide, two are rather general explanations of violent behavior already mentioned above sec. 1. They are

1. The frustration-aggression theory
2. The subculture of violence theory

The third theory is simply Durkheim's theory of suicide.

Bohannan (1960) likewise suggested that Durkheim's theory of suicide could also be used to explain homicide. In other words one should explain homicide in terms of the state of integration and regulation of the social system (cp. sec. 5). In particular the condition of reduced regulation or anomie was seen as not only suicidal, but also as the most important homicidal category.

Homicide involves at least two persons: a killer and a victim, anomie may characterize one of these only or both.

No attempt was made to subject the anomic theory to a formal test. It was noted in section 1 that the explanatory power of the frustration-aggression theory seemed questionable. The subculture of violence approach seems closer to facts but is still too general and vague in its predictions.

It is therefore likely that Durkheim's theory is the best sociological explanation of homicide available at present. However, as for suicide, an ecological approach admitting both sociological and personal factors may be preferable for predictive purposes.

Sociological factors would still be quite dominant because social conditions are major instigators and maintainers of human aggression (cf. Bandura 1973, p. 181).

7. Hierarchical Violence

«In the same way then an expert in any art avoids excess and deficiency, and seeks and adopts the mean — the mean, that is, not of the thing but relative to us».

Aristotle (Nichomachean Ethics II, VI 8)

. . . «and that man is by nature a political animal» . . .
Aristotle, Politics, I,I,9.

7.1 Mass Violence

It was documented in section 3 that accidental death, suicide, and homicide possess certain common characteristics which were revealed in internal correlations and in similar relationship to certain external factors. The three types of operational violence are rather individual in occurrence, at most a small group is involved. In contrast hierarchical violence and territorial violence frequently involve large masses of people. The hierarchical variety is limited by the national border, while the territorial violence may range widely.

Most theorists and researchers have treated the two mass violence types most frequently termed «revolution» and «war» as quite separate phenomena. An exception is found in Timasheff's book from 1965 which is called War and Revolution. Timasheff was Sorokin's assistant in the collection of Sorokin's data on revolutions, and he was, like Sorokin, a Russian by birth and present in Russia at least up to around the October revolution 1917.

Timasheff contends that it is possible to state three abstract conditions which must be present for either revolution or war to occur. These three conditions may be summarized as follows:

1. Serious conflict
2. Peaceful means rejected by at least one part
3. Each party to the conflict expects to have an even chance to win

The serious conflicts are seen by Timasheff as in principle controlable. Thus in regard to territorial conflicts he suggested an international organization with a recognized right to adjust disputed borders. In regard to revolutions they can by principle 3 be prevented by maintaining a strong government meeting violence by superior violence if necessary. His cure for revolutions seems more realistic and within reach. His cure for war really presupposes a level of cosmopolitan cooperation not yet reached.

In terms of demographic categories wars have tended to expose the male population to a heightened risk of violent death. The most exposed categories seem to have been males aged 15—29, and among their generation the upper half in regard to physical fitness (see in particular Chesnais 1976, pp. 192—197). For constant age the risk of death in war is normally higher for officers than for men (cf. Dumas & Vedel-Petersen 1922).

Hierarchical violence victims seem also to be sampled with higher than average intensity among young males and here too the higher than average in social status seem to be more highly exposed (Laquere 1968).

7.2 Sorokin on Internal Disturbances

The term hierarchical violence is here used to refer to all kinds of violence which occur during more or less organized or more or less comprehensive internal disturbances within a society. It is meant to comprise the same set of behaviors which Sorokin designated as internal disturbances and gave a violence score above 1. Although the primary emphasis here will be on that part of such disturbances which has lethal consequences, it is particularly desirable for the study of long-time trends to use the broader definition, derived from Sorokin, since he is the major source. The data may be said to represent what other authors may have referred to as civic strife, public disorders, or revolution. In the case of hierarchical violence it is particularly important to observe that only a very small part of all violent events under this general category refer to revolutions and that a still smaller part refer to the more well-known revolutions: the English revolution in the seventeenth century, the French in the eighteenth-century, and the Russian in the twentieth-century. However, if attention is limited to lethal violence, revolutions will probably constitute a greater part of the total. It does not seem possible to be more precise, because the relevant data in most cases do not exist but have to be inferred. Sorokin's work on internal disturbances covered Europe from the Middle Ages up to c. 1925 and in addition a 1000 years history of Greece and Rome, altogether a period from 600 B.C. to 1925 A. D.

Sorokin used three indicators in his study of internal disturbances

1. Number of disturbances
2. Number of years with disturbances
3. Total score taking several factors into account.

(see Tables 7.1a, 7.1b showing data for France from 525 to 1925, and for England from the seventh-century onwards.

The two first-mentioned indicators need no further explanation. But the total score will need a brief explanation.

Sorokin scored all internal disturbances in each of 11 nations or nation groups according to areal diffusion, duration, population involved, and violence involved. None of these scores refer to precise amounts of space, time, population and deaths but rather to varying amounts that are given rank scores. Thus the score is 1 if disturbance is highly local, e.g. only in one county, and 100 if the whole national area is involved. Durations likewise start with 1 for momentary events, and 100 for duration 25 years or more:

1 year gives a score of	10
5 years gives a score of	30
15 years gives a score of	70
25 years or more gives a score of	100

Population involved is ranked in five categories. Violence is likewise ranked in five categories: the lowest, scored 1, indicates a disturbance without violence (p. 395); higher scores indicate increasing degrees of violence and «political changes». When the latter two scores are combined into a mass-intensity score, they are first separately rescored so that the 1 to 5 scores are changed to 1, 3, 5, 7, and 10 on each of the two variables. They are then multiplied and results are rounded off to the nearest digit divisable by 5, except when one or both scores are 1, in which case no rounding off takes place.

The final measure of disturbance is the geometric average of three scores: the area score, the duration score, and the population — violence score.

X geom = (Area score x Duration score x Population-violence score)$^{1/3}$

Example: Disturbance No. 131 happened in England 1641—1649. Its name is The Great Revolution. It is scored as follows by Sorokin:

Social Area	Duration	Population	Violence	PV[1]	Xgeom
100	46	5	5	100	77

The score of 77 shows[2] that this was a major disturbance. It spread to the entire nation, it comprised the total population, it was among the most violent, and it lasted 9 years. A duration of 25 years or more would have given the maximum average score of 100.

In France in the year 605 there was an insurrection among the Burgundian nobles:

Area	20
Duration	5
Population	2
Violence	3
Population times Violence	15
Geom, average: $(20 \times 4 \times 15)^{1/3}$	11.45

This was a local disturbance of only 6 months' duration involving only a part of the total population and not very violent. The score becomes 12 indicating a minor uprising.

Tables similar to Table 7.1 were produced for Germany-Austria, England, Italy, Spain, Netherlands, Russia, and Poland-Lithuania. In addition there are tables for Greece, Rome, and Byzantium.

Sorokin's summary list (p. 474, Table 48) of «important social disturbances» covers 11 nations or nation groups and the total of years studied (summation for all eleven units) is 11,978 nation-years containing altogether 1629 disturbances, giving a mean time of 7.35 years between disturbances. The disturbances were most densely spaced in time in Greece (5.4) and least densely spaced in Byzantium (17.5); the Netherlands was next in density with 12.1. The average ratio of years without to years with disturbances was lowest in Spain and highest in Byzantium with France as next highest. The Byzantium data could according to Sorokin be deviant because of more limited source material (ibid. p. 473).

7.3 Trend

In most European nations studied by Sorokin the peak of internal disturbances is most likely to be found in the late Middle Ages (eleventh to fifteenth-centuries) and the lowest levels of such activity are most likely to be discovered in the sixteenth to nineteenth centuries. In fact several nations seem to approach a kind of steady state of moderate or low disturbance rate after the year 1500.

This steady state of moderate or low disturbances rates has continued into the twentieth century in most European states.

Bank's series for successful coups d'état or revolutions 1815—1966 showed a steady state of no such event throughout the period for the United Kingdom. France had no such event after 1870 but 5 events altogether all in the period 1830—1970. Germany (Prussia) had only 1 event (1919). USSR (Russia) also only one (1919). USA had no such event 1815—1966 and Japan only one (1968). China is exceptional with 7 successful events between 1861 and 1949.

Table 7.1a Internal Disturbances (Sorokin 1937) France

Century	Number of disturbances	Number of years with disturbance	Total Score
6	7	9	85
7	5	13	86
8	6	13	143
9	6	14	135
10	4	5	35
11	9	27	142
12	25	37	289
13	21	39	245
14	11	10	117
15	10	11	95
16	13	30	197
17	18	24	197
18	13	32	203
19	23	21	235
20 (1901—1925)	2	2	29

Table 7.1b England

Century	Number of disturbances	Number of years with disturbance	Total Score
7	7	10	99
8	28	31	288
9	12	18	182
10	12	14	138
11	12	16	182
12	7	22	101
13	11	21	187
14	12	14	161
15	15	28	302
16	12	15	129
17	17	27	209
18	10	11	102
19	10	12	76
20	1	3	29

However for the major powers of Europe, for the USA and for Japan, it seems to be possible to assert that industrialization and urbanization has favored the powers in command of the government, making a successful revolution a rare event.

Tilly (1969) published comparable data on hierarchical violence in France 1830—1860 and 1930—1960. The total number estimated to be killed or wounded for 1830—1860 was 16319 and for 1930—1960:16,435. When population size 1840 and 1940 is taken into account, the earlier period shows an average number killed or wounded per year and per million population of 16 and the later period 12.

From a sampling of American newspaper reports on political violence 1819—1968 Kirkham et al. (1969) concluded that the total number of deaths thus registered was 27 for the years 1819—1848, 372 for the years 1849—1878, 440 for the years 1879—1908, 180 for the years 1909—1938, and 90 for the years 1939—1968.

Taking population size into account these figures produce a declining series since about 1850.[3] The decline may even be underestimated because the older newspapers had lower reporting capacity (cf. also Levy 1969).

It was shown in section 2 that both France and England suffered very few deaths from hierarchical violence in the first 6/10 of the twentieth century.

Germany experienced considerable violence during the Hitler era, and the Russian revolution and its aftermath made an enormous contribution to the death toll in Russia.

Considering the more recent past (1948—1967), Tailors' and Hudson's data on deaths from domestic violence 1948—1967 produced a declining series for the United Kingdom, Germany, China, and Japan, but an increasing series for France, USSR and USA.

However, Gurr's important analysis of civil strife in the world in the 1960s documented rather sharply the reduced death toll from civil strife among highly developed nations (Gurr 1969) as compared with less developed nations.

Gurr estimated that a sample of 114 nations studied over the period 1961—1965 had experienced a death toll from civil strife corresponding to 238 deaths per million population, or about 50 deaths per year per million from this cause.

Civil strife during this period was about 500 times more deadly in 38 nations at a low economic level than in 37 nations at a high economic level (Table 17—10, p. 461).

Gurr presented estimates of deaths per million population from civil strife over the five years 1961—65 (USA 1963—68) as follows:

	Deaths 1961—65 per million population
All nations (114)	238
Nations by economic development:	
High (37)[4]	2
Medium (32)	264
Low (69)	841
Nations by geocultural region:	
European (37)[5]	2
Latin(24)	76
Islamic (21)	222
Asian (17)	357
African (25)	539

Gurr's figures when divided by 5 give the annual death rate from civil strife 1961—1965. For the European nations the average becomes .4 individuals per year per million population or about 40 per million deaths.

Gurr & McClelland (1971, p. 27) measured the magnitude of civil strife in 12 nations ca. 1927—1936 and ca. 1957—1966. One half of the nations were Western European. The average scores on all indicators used declined from the first period to the second as follows:

	Mean score	
	First decennium	Second decennium
Turmoil	51	25
Conspiracy	10	7
Internal War	30	8
Sum	91	40

It seems necessary to conclude that the weight of evidence available favors the theory of declining internal imbalance violence with increasing industrialization.

Tocqueville (1961) predicted the trend here asserted to exist and labeled one of his chapters in *Democracy in America* «Why Great Revolutions will become more rare».

7.4 Demographic Cost and Amount of Change

As already mentioned, hierarchical violence includes all cases of revolutionary violence and all other types of internal disturbance accompanied by violent behavior.

Within the field of hierarchical violence this study seeks to center on lethal violence. The aim is to discover factors that may account for more or less deadly behavior when internal disturbances occur.

In contrast the objective of most theorists dealing with internal disturbances is to explain revolutionary behavior and the amount of social changes caused by such behavior.

Operational violence deaths in the Western World tend to kill 500—1000 persons per million population per year in the Western World. Compared to this figure most revolutions listed by Tanter & Midlarsky (1967) for the period 1955—1960 are modest killers. In fact among 18 successful revolutions listed only seven cost more than one hundred deaths per million per year, and none cost as much as 500 deaths per million population per year.

Cohan (1975) reviewed several «theories of revolution» and concluded that the emphasis on violence was only one out of six dimensions that had been proposed, although a frequently used dimension. Cohan himself seemed most inclined to leave violence out of revolutionary theory, partly because it is difficult to study empirically, but partly because it would allow concentration on the changes caused by the revolutin. As Dahrendorf (1961) noted: revolutions are changes that are not only violent and rapid but also influential. It is therefore quite reasonable for theorists of revolutions to concentrate on the structural effects rather than on their demographic cost. But eo ipso they become less relevant to the study of internal disturbances as a cause of death. For this reason the fairly large literature on revolutionary behavior will receive a rather selective attention. In the following analysis theoretical contributions have been classified according to major suggested causes or correlates of hierarchical violence or of revolutions. Five causes were noted: Inequality, Rate of change, Technology, Contagion, and Repression.

7.5 Inequality, Heterogeneity, Dissensus

Plato (427—347) may be among the first analysts of social systems to stress inequality as an imbalancing factor in such systems (Republic part 4 § 3). Extreme wealth is said to lead to luxury, idleness, and a passion for novelty. Extreme poverty is held to produce meanness, inferior workmanship, and «revolution into the bargain» (p. 422, Penguin ed. 1959).

Aristotle (384—322) discussed the causes of revolution in his Politics (chapter 5), where he stresses that social unrest is conditioned by a desire for equality. In the Nichomachean Ethics he further emphasized equality as an essential element of friendship. Machiavelli (1515) in his work *The Prince* pointed out that a prince has a more risky position in a nation divided into an elite of lords and a mass of commoners. He mentioned France as a country of lords and masses and Turkey as a country where everybody was a devout subject of the prince (chapter 4). He returned to similar considerations in chapter 9, where the prince was warned against receiving the crown from the hand of some nobles rather than obtaining it with the aid of the people.

Tocqueville (1961, 1951, 1835) likewise pointed to inequality as the fountain of revolutionary activity: «Remove the secondary causes that have produced the great convulsions of the world and you will almost always find the principle of inequality at the bottom. Either the poor have attempted to plunder the rich or the rich to enslave the poor».

With transition from aristocratic to democratic community the poor change from being an immense majority of have-nots to a small minority enjoying improved legal status. The wealthy are few and powerless. Between these two extremes is found in a democracy an «innumerable multitude of men almost alike». These people possess enough to desire order.

Although Vierkandt (1922) is somewhat vague in his analysis of the causes of revolutions, he does mention possible factors like «a newly awakened» self-consciousness in the lower classes, and serious interior or exterior defects, which at any rate contain the germs both of the inequality theme and the rate of change theme.

Edwards (1970, 1927, pp. 69—70) considered that «no great revolution has ever succeeded without the assistance of the economic incentive». There is according to Edwards discontent with poverty and envy of the rich by the poor in every society.

Russett (1971, 1964) produced data from 47 nations on inequality in landownership and indicators of political instability and violence.

In particular his Gini index measuring degree of inequality correlated .46 with the number of violent political deaths per million.

Good (1966) pointed to barriers against upward social mobility as a potent cause of revolution.

Tanter & Midlarsky (1967) compared land inequality (Gini index) and incidence of successful revolution for 50 nations. The result may be summarized in a 2×2 table:

	Successful revolution	No successful revolution
Gini index .75 or higher	9	13
Below .75	1	27
	10	40

Since a high Gini index indicates a high level of inequality, the data support the theories that connect revolution with inequality.

Baechler (1970) pointed to dissensus on basic values, heterogeneity of customs, and inequality in regard to power, wealth, and prestige as factors tending to disturb the normal operation of social mechanisms for the non-violent settlement of conflicts.

Hibbs (1973) appraoched the problem of the causation of internal imbalance through a multiple regression analysis of a sample of 108 nations for whom data on collective protest activity and more violent disorders were available. His findings refer to the years around 1960.

In Hibbs' final model four variants of internal violence stand in the center of attention:

1. Collective Protest, a non-lethal activity
2. Internal War, armed attacks, deaths, assassination
3. Repression by government
4. Coups by counter elites

The first two are related by a correlation of .63.

The path going from Repression to Internal War has the highest path coefficient in the entire model: .8. Repression and Protests hang together through mutual determination of size .5. The Coups stand more isolated from the rest but are positively affecting Repression and positively, although weakly, affected by Internal War.

Let us inquire further what the model suggests as generating these variants of internal imbalance. In regard to Internal War, which in the present context is the most important variable, only two such generators are suggested. One has to do with the type of government and indicates that internal war is more likely in the non-Communist than in the Communist part of the world. The other variable is termed Separatism and is measured as percentage dissatsified with the closeness of their ties to the total social system. Internal war is thus somewhat more likely where the population is heterogeneous in such basic matters, as race, religion, language, and or other customs.

Theorists have disagreed as to which position on the economic inequality variable would be most conducive to political violence within a nation (Sigelman & Simpson 1977). Some writers seem to assume a linear relatinship meaning that violence will be most likely for a maximum level of inequality. At least one writer mentioned by Sigelman & Simpson (Davis 1948) made a plea for a curvilinear theory with a dip in the middle, claiming that revolutinary movements are most likely toward the extremes of economic distribution rather than at the middle stages. Still another view may be derived from considerations of the appearance of deprivation comparisons, which Nagel (1974) conceived of as becoming more frequent with decreasing income inequality. The amount of discontent, however, was expected to increase with inequality, and thus a curvilinear hypothesis is formulated where the most violence-provoking point is for some middle value of inequality.

In their study of 49 nations Sigelman & Simpson (1977) found no support for the curvilinear theories but did confirm the linear relationship between a measure of the incidence of «internal war» and economic inequality as measured by the Gini index ($R_{\text{Int. War; In Population, Gini index}} = .46$)

Zipf (1950) suggested in one of his latest papers that a cooperative and harmonious organization would tend to distribute wages according to a definite principle:

$$\log y = k - \frac{1}{2} \log x, \text{ where}$$

y = hourly wage
x = number employed at that wage
k = a constant

Deviations from the straight line relationship (in the logarithms) with slope — 1/2 should, according to Zipf, be seen as danger signals suggesting imminent risk of «destructive rivalry».

7.6 Rate of Change

Machiavelli (1515) referred in several chapters to the importance of the rate of social change in regard to the risk of a revolution. This occurred perhaps most directly in chapter 6, where he issued a warning to the effect that nothing is more dangerous than to introduce a completely new governmental policy. Nor is it in chapter 7 considered without risk to come too suddenly to power or in general to be a newcomer to power (chapter 2). But a slow rate of change can also be an added risk. When it comes to repressive violence, it should be concentrated in time rather than diffused over a longer time (chapter 7).

Although Marx and Engels (1848) stressed inequality as a basic condition for social unrest, they did not consider inequality potent enough to produce revolutions without facilitating factors. Thus Marx (1850) flatly declared that no revolution could occur under conditions of general prosperity when the productive forces are as richly developed as conditions of bourgeois society allow.

Marx (1859) wrote in the preface to his Political Economy as follows:

«Aut einer gewissen Stufe ihrer Entvicklung geraten die materiellen Produktivkräfte der Gesellschaft in Widerspruch mit den vorhandenen Pro-
duktionsverhältnissen oder, was nur ein juristischer Ausdruck dafür ist, mit
den Eigentumsverhältnissen, innerhalb derer sie sich bisher bewegt hatten.
Aus Entwicklungsformen der Produktivkräfte schlagen diese Verhältnisse in
Fesseln derselben um. Es tritt dann eine Epoche sozialer Revolution ein».

Ellwood (1905) was quite explicit in his explanation of social revolutions. The
invariant situation is one of differential rates of change, although these words
were not used.

Ellwood says that societies where the social habits and institutions become
inflexible are «bound to have trouble». This is so because the «conditions of
social life» change rapidly. Sooner or later such habits will break down.

If they are habits connected with social control, a revolution will occur.

Geiger (1926, pp. 57, 58) stressed the rapid change in evaluations in
modern civilization as against the slow change in social structures whereby a
discrepancy developed between the ideal society and the actual society. This
creates a tension which he termed revolutionary situation. The revolution has
the effect that the actual society by changing rapidly corresponds thereafter
to the development of the ideology and its ideal society.

Sorokin (1928) explained the occurrence of revolutions in general as due to
oppression of instincts and to governmental inefficiency. Hunger, a war
involving serious human losses, political suppression to the extent that they
affect a large proportion of a population make the population revolution-
prone. But a further qualitification is that not absolute positions but rather
relative positions are important. For the revolution to succeed it is also
necessary that the government fails to measure up to the task of either
suppressing or channelizing or dissipating the revolutionary energy.

Sorokin's (1928) ideas may reasonably be interpreted as a variant of social
change theory, since the social processes responsible for the oppression of
instincts (hunger, war, repression, etc.) may proceed at a rapid rate, e.g. in
terms of numbers killed, wounded, sick, or imprisoned per day as against a
slow rate of ameliorative activity by the government.

Sorokin (1937) explained internal disturbances as follows: . . .«the main
and the indispensable condition for an eruption of internal disturbances is
that the social system or the cultural system or both shall be unsettled»
(p. 499).

He further stressed that the transitional periods from Ideational to Sensate
or vice versa in some or all fields of culture or social relations were just such
unsettling conditions tending to produce «rising tides of disturbances» (ibid
p. 505).

Olson (1971, 1963) stressed the importance of the rate of economic change: «It is not those who are accustomed to poverty, but those whose place in the social order is changing, who resort to revolution». Economic growth creates or increases the category of «nouveau riches» and may also produce «noveaux pauvres», and both these categories will be more interested in social and political change than the stable parts of the population.

Rapid economic growth is a «disruptive and destabilizing force that leads to political instability».

Chirot & Ragin (1975) investigated the differential participation in the Roumanian peasant revolt in March 1907. Although the sample size used was modest (32 Roumanian counties), the correlations and regression coefficient found proved a strong and convincing support for one of two competing theories of peasant revolts tested.

The most predictive theory proved to be one stressing at least implicitly differential rates of change: the high rate of commercialization of agriculture as measured by prevalence of wheat cultivation versus the low rate of change in the attitudes of farmers as inferred from the prevailing high rate of rural illiteracy (average percent illiterate:84).

In fact the simple correlation coefficient between a measure of the number of deaths per county and the product of the commercialization measure and the traditionalism measure was .85(N = 32).

Davies (1962, 1969, 1973, 1974) presented a theory of revolution which contains the central assumption that a common element in the pre-revolutionary situation is a downward bend of a need satisfaction curve which for some time has followed a steady upwards course.

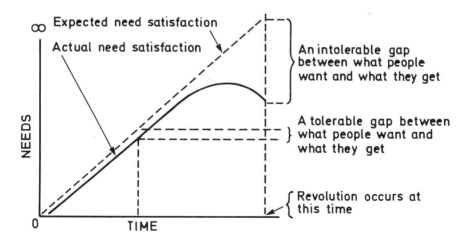

Fig. 7.1 Need satisfaction and revolution. From Davies (1973). Reprinted by permission.

The assumption combined ideas from Marx (downward bend) and from Tocqueville (upward course) (see Tocqueville, English 1955 ed., pp. 174—177).

Reviewing his theory Davies (1973) emphasized as his view that violence is always a response to frustration but only one of many such responses. Violence is only the outcome if innate needs are deeply frustrated.

Davies documented that some major revolutionary changes had been preceded by the conditions specified by his theory. It remains to establish how many non-revolutionary changes were preceded by the same conditions (cf. also Davies 1974). Davies theory is a variant of the frustrationaggression theories discussed above (sec. 1).

Graham & Gurr (1969, pp. 621—644) stressed the importance of «men's frustration over some of the material and social circumstances of their lives» as a necessary precondition of group protest and collective violence.

Gurr (1969) produced a number of correlations with civil strife tending to confirm Davies' theory.

Feierabend & Feierabend (1966) concluded on the basis of empirical findings that modern nations tend to be more stable because they possess greater ability to meet the demands of their citizens. The less advanced nations are less stable. This may be explained by a higher level of frustration, but the authors add that reduced stability may also be seen as a consequence of higher rate of change of social systems.

Actually the authors test and confirm both these explanations.

The more unstable social systems had both more frustrated populations and were subject to higher rates of change in several important social and economic variables. A Pearson $r = .65$ was found between a measure of political instability 1955—1961 and a measure of rate of modernization 1935—1962.

Modernization variables were chiefly measures of education, standard of living, and urbanization. Feierabend, Feierabend & Nesvold (1969) emphasized the importance of one particular type of differential change rates to political violence. The combination of rapid increase in educational level and a smaller increase in per capita income was seen as a virulent mixture of conditions.Thus American urban disorders in the 1960s are explained as a «gap between education and income, between aspirations and satisfaction».

Both these authors and Gurr formulated their psychological interpretation of differential change rates and violence in terms of the frustration-aggression approach (cf. sec. 1).

Baechler (1970) stressed that revolutionary phenomena are more likely to appear with economic prosperity than with economic crisis and referred to Capareto's Traité § 2566[6]. The explanation is seen in the tendency of economic

114

growth to create some dysfunctions and some suffering.

Baechler also noted the positive impact given to revolutionary movements by sudden depressions as against the absence of correlation between degree of misery and revolutionary behavior.

Defeat in war was also mentioned as a condition favoring revolutionary actiivty.

Galtung (1974) presented a theory of revolutions, the main content of which seems to be a listing of factors that are generally favorable to the activities of revolutionaries. One of the factors listed was Davies' frustrated expectation. Frustration in Galtung's theory comes from rank disequilibrium among top-dogs and from underdog suffering. Still more factors are needed to explain revolutions. These are in Galtung's formulation chiefly organizational factors: organized interaction, appropriate ideology, charismatic leadership, and revolutionary strategy.

7.7 Technology

The general downward trend in the occurrence of hierarchical violence in the Western World seems to be favored by the growth of science and technology. This factor may also explain the considerably higher level of hierarchical violence in the less developed nations. An advanced technology seems also to favor the political pluralism of the Western Europe-Northern America type.

Baechler (1970) regarded a pluralistic regime as a protection against revolution, whereas the political alternative and much more common regime in the present world and in the past, a monopolistic regime, was considered highly vulnerable to revolutionary movements, because of a rather general tendency of such regimes to become inefficient and incompetent (pp. 181—182).

7.8 Contagion

There seems to be considerable support for the view that revolutionary activity or social upheavals occur in waves. This was the case in South America 1943—1953 and also in the Soviet zone 1956. Huntington (1962) related these observations to the contagiousness of this kind of activity and to the efficient and fast methods for the diffusion of news. Spilerman (1976), similarly, explained the spread of the 1967 urban disorders in the United States as a product of contagion, in particular through television.

Stohl (1975) analyzed domestic political violence in the USA 1890—1970 and found in general only a very modest correlation or no correlation at all between the number killed in civil disorders and the condition of the total social system as belligerent or as non-belligerent. Pitcher, Hamblin & Miller (1978) developed a simple push and pull model to represent tendencies towards imitating violence and towards inhibition of such activity.

Their model had the following variables:
p = proportion of accumulated number of imitations
q = proportion of accumulated inhibitions
I = number of imitations
i = number of inhibitions
V = accumulated number of acts of violence

Equations:

(1) $\dfrac{dI}{dt} = pI$ Hence $\dfrac{dI}{I} = pdt$

(2) $\dfrac{di}{dt} = qi$ Hence $\dfrac{di}{i} = q\,dt$

(3) $i = i_o e^{qt}$, by integration of (2)

(4) $\dfrac{dV}{V} = \dfrac{p}{i}\,dt$

When (3) is inserted in (4) we obtain:

(5) $\dfrac{dV}{V} = \dfrac{pdt}{i_o e^{qt}} = ce^{-qt}dt$

where $c = \dfrac{p}{i_o}$

It will be seen that the relative growth of violence increases with p, which measures unit strength of imitation, but decreases with q which measures unit strength of inhibition. Furthermore, the relative increment is c for $t = 0$, and the system reaches a steady and maximum state (for $t > 0$) for $t = +\infty$ when relative change becomes zero.

Integration of equation 5 produces the Gompertz equation

6) $V = Ae^{kb^t}$
where $c = -qk$ and $q = -\ln b$

Using equation 6, they documented that the accumulated incidence of many types of violence could be described rather closely by the model, but the number of observations in each test seems to have been fairly small.

The equation described the accumulated number of lynchings of blacks in the United States 1882—1956, of several lynching incidents on the American continent 1967—1973, as well as of various riots, coups, and civil disorders from different parts of the world both recent and as far back in time as 1830.

Inhibition as measured by q was shown to correlate highly ($r^2 = .97$) with duration of violent outbreak measured in days.

7.9 Repression

The efficiency of revolutionary efforts will have to compete with the efficiency of governmental repression. A major factor in repressive efficiency is the ability to present the revolutionaries with a sufficiently overwhelming counterforce. The defending government should have a numerical superiority of at least 10:1, in some situations as much as 100:1 to beat the offensive forces. This is characacteristic of civil disordes as opposed to wars. In civil disorders the defensive position is the more difficult task; in war the difficult task is the offensive role, where traditional military lore demands at least three-to-one majority for success (Huntington 1962).

Pareto (1963, 1916) in his § 2057 clearly placed a major emphasis on the repressive morale of the ruling elite.

If the ruling elite was poorly motivated for efficient use of force relative to the non-elite, a revolution would take place.

Such morale deficiency in the ruling elite was explained as due either to insufficient vertical mobility or to other not further specified causes.

For a similar emphasis see Timasheff (1965). Johnson (1964) stressed the strength of the status quo defenders, because the application of science to warfare has created a tool for the government which is invincible to any force not similarly equipped and trained. In Brinton's (1952, 1938) analysis of the English, American, French, and Russian revolutions, one of the common factors favoring the revolutionaries was governmental inefficiency and low morale among the ruling elite and among the military forces. Such demoralization is particularly noticeable in reports of military behavior after defeat in war.

Baechler (1970) pointed to three factors which normally tended to keep the number and rate of success of revolutionary attempts down:

1) The numerical superiority of the defending (= repressing) forces
2) The material superiority of the defence
3) The superior discipline of the defending military forces

Tilly (1975) contended that European domestic warfare is invariably characterized by a higher rate of killing and wounding by the defenders or repressive forces. In return the power-seekers or revolutionaries do most of the property damage. Tilly also stressed the normally strong advantage of the repressive forces in terms of arms and military discipline.

For the measurement of governmental repression in an analysis of deadly violence, the only acceptable measure is the number of deaths caused by such repression or measures correlating highly with number of deaths by repression. Such measures do not seem to exist. Still, it would seem plausible, that at measure of freedom of the press should be negatively correlated with repressive deaths.

The measure of freedom of the press tabulated by Taylor & Hudson (1972, Table 2.7) ran from a score of -4 to a score of $+4$.

The average score for China and the USSR was -3.1, while the United Kingdom, France, West Germany, USA, and Japan obtained an average score of $+2.4$

Hence the difference between East and West is 69% of the maximum possible difference on this scale. It seems plausible to expect a higher level also of the stronger degrees of repression in countries where freedom of the press is severely limited.

8. Territorial Violence

8.1 Sorokin on War

Sorokin studied the incidence of war and revolution within a part of Western civilization (European part) from 600 BC to 1925 AD. For each war he tried to estimate

    a) strength of the army
    b) number of casualties (killed, wounded or missing)
    c) the duration of war

He studied Greece, Rome, Austria, Germany, England, France, the Netherlands, Spain, Italy, Russia, and Poland-Lithuania. Duration of war is known in almost all cases.

More specifically Sorokin reported on war duration and casualties by quarter century for Greece − 500 to − 126, for Rome − 400 to 476, for France 976—1925, Russia 900—1925, England 1051—1925, Austria-Hungary 951—1925, Germany 1651—1925, Italy 1551—1925, Spain 1476—1925, Holland 1551—1925, Poland and Lithuania 1386—1800.

Sorokin's report on his study of war is quite concentrated. Although he deals with both theories and facts in rgard to wars covering about 2000 years of European history, the part of his Social and Cultural Dynamics dealing with war covers only 160 pages.

Sorokin's main problem in his study of war is the scarcity of data for most of the period of investigation. He consequently decided to start by securing information or estimates of

    1) the duration of a war, and
    2) the size of the army

The information on duration is usually quite reliable, at least compared to other war information. In contrast, reports on most wars before 1600 contain no reliable information on the number of wounded, dead or missing. Sorokin contends, however, that even under such conditions estimates may be produced that are likely to be within the range possible at the time of the war. Once an estimate of army size (A) is available, the army size for a war of duration t years is estimated as $tA = A_t$. Furthermore, casualties are generally not reported in a reliable fashion — if figures are mentioned at all. Sorokin contends, however, that in the few cases where reliable accounts are available, casualties[1] (C) tend to be proportional to army size $C = kA_t = ktA$ with 100 k ranging between 2 and 6. This range included American relative war losses in the Spanish American War, and in World War 1.

Thus the Greek-Persian War lasted from -475 to -451. Hence $t = 25$. Average annual army strength is assumed to be: $A = 20,000$. Hence $tA = 500,000$ for the 25-year period. 100 k = 6 (assumption based on report of 6% casualities in a battle in the year 458 B.C.).

$$C = .06 \times 500,000 = 30,000$$

An example from the Middle Ages:

France fought a war with England 1324—1325. With expected army size given as 5,000, $tA = 2 \times 5,000 = 10,000$. Casualty rate is assumed to be .02. Hence total number of casualties becomes 200.

Sorokin next accumulated casualties for a nation or nation group for quarter-centuries and centuries. The latter figures, i.e. casualties for centuries, are divided through by population (P) estimates as of the middle of the century concerned and then multiplied by 10^6

$$I_x = \frac{\sum_{i=1}^{100} C_{ix} 10^6}{P_{(x-1/2)}}$$

It will be seen that I_x may be considered an approximation to the following formula:

$$I_x = \frac{10^2 \bar{C}_x 10^6}{\bar{P}_x}$$

where $\bar{C}_x$ = annual average casuality for century x and P_x is population annual average in century X.

It will be noted that
I_x is proportional
to the mean per capita and per annum casuality.

Thus if Ix is divided by 100, we obtain an estimate of annual casualities per million population.

Sorokin's values for the twentieth century are only based on 25 years of observation. To obtain an average casualty rate by year we should divide total accumulated casualties by 25 not 100 as done by Sorokin, whose twentieth century estimates are consequently 1/4 of the ones here presented. Sorokin's index may be compared with Richardson's index.

$$\text{Sorokin } I_x = 10^8 \frac{\overline{C}_x}{\overline{P}_x}$$

Richardson

$$R_x = \frac{\overline{\ddot{K}}_x}{\overline{D}_x}$$

$\overline{K}_x$ = mean number killed per year in period x

$\overline{D}_x$ = mean number of deaths per year in period X

$\overline{K} = \alpha \overline{C}_x$

$\overline{D}_x = \beta \overline{P}_x$

It follows that $I_x = 10^8 \dfrac{\overline{Cx}}{\overline{Px}} = 10^8 R_x \dfrac{\beta}{\alpha}$

and $R_x = I_x 10^{-8} \dfrac{\alpha}{\beta}$

Sorokin (1928) p. 291) assumes in general, conforming to earlier researchers, that there are 3 to 4 wounded for each battle death. With a ratio $1:3\cdot5$ we have $\alpha = .22 = \dfrac{1}{4.5}$

With an annual mortality of 2 percent

$\beta = .02$

and

$$R_x = \frac{\overline{K}_x}{\overline{D}_x} = \frac{.22\overline{C}_x}{.02\overline{P}_x} \quad 11x \frac{\overline{C}_x}{\overline{P}_x} \doteq I_x x 10^{-7}$$

121

8.2 Trend

In sharp contrast to the declining trend observed for hierarchical violence, the trend for territorial violence is, at least in Europe, definitely a growing function of time. Even the nineteenth century relatively peaceful in comparison with the seventeenth and eighteenth centuries, seems to have seen more war casualties per capita than any of the centuries from the twelfth to the sixteenth. (Tables 8.1, 8.2 both from Sorokin.)

Table 8.1 Casualty rate by century. France, Great Britain, Austria, Hungary, Russia.
Adapted from Sorokin 1937, Vol. 3, p. 345, Table 19.

Century	Population $\times 10^{-6}$	$\dfrac{\text{Annual casualties}}{\text{Mean population}} \times 10^6$
12	13—10	23— 30
13	18—13	38— 53
14	25—18	66— 93
15	35—25	81—114
16	45—35	127—164
17	55	454
18	90	402
19	172	170
20	305	2118

Table 8.2 Casualty rate by century. England, France, Germany, Russia.
Adapted from Sorokin (1937, p. 349 Table 20).

$\dfrac{\text{Annual mean number of casualties}}{\text{mean population}} 10^6$

Nation	Century			
	17	18	19	20 (first quarter)
England	200	301	50	665 × 4
France	366	458	510	920 × 4
Germany	—	—	131	947 × 4
Russia	79	215	111	411 × 4

Note: Twentieth-century entries are four times higher than those given by Sorokin. Cf. above.

A central problem is, of course, the validity of Sorokin's estimates. It will be contended that independent evidence confirms Sorokin's finding of a long-term increase in war casualties. The most important corroboration comes from Wright's study of war (1965, 1942). Wright's study is the most comprehensive analysis of the possible causes and correlates of wars. His detailed listing of European war activity covers the period 1485—1940. His tabulation of battles by centuries is particularly useful, because it documents independently from Sorokin the increasing violence of modern times (Table 8.3).

Table 8.3 Number of battles fought by France, Austria, Great Britain, Russia, Prussia, Spain, Netherlands, Sweden, Denmark, and Turkey 1500—1940. (Wright Table 23, p. 628).

	Total no. of battles
1500—1549	52
1550—1599	79
1600—1649	201
1650—1699	282
1700—1749	640
1750—1799	993
1800—1849	946
1850—1899	263
1900—1940	1254

Wright noted a number of trends in regard to the wars in the Western World since c. 1500. Armies became larger, the duration of battles and their number per time unit and per war increased.[2] Because of these trends Wright contended that the number of battle deaths had also increased even relative to population (cf. op.cit. p. 242 and section 2.3).

Richardson tried to register all deaths 1820—1945 due to participation in some kind of deadly quarrel resulting in one or more deaths. Richardson judged that his list of such quarrels leading to $10^{3.5}$ deaths or more was complete or nearly so. He was aware, however, (p. 31) of the possibility that some large wars in Africa 1820—1860 might be missing. He also assumed that his count of quarrels producing between $10^{3.5}$ and 10^{5} deaths was incomplete (p. 153). The count had produced 188 such quarrels. A straight line interpolation suggested the figure 2530, which Richardson considered unlikely, preferring a curvilinear interpolation giving the figure 354.

Since Richardson's count of war and war deaths is without doubt closer to truth for large wars with more than $10^{3.5}$ deaths than for small wars, a table (p. 141) showing wars of this size in the world 1820—1884 and 1885—1949 is of particular interest. It gives the following result:

| | Deadly quarrels ending in year | |
Number of deaths	1820—1884	1885—1949
$10^{4 \cdot 5} - 10^{7 \cdot 5}$	12	23
$10^{3 \cdot 5} - 10^{4 \cdot 5}$	38	32
Total with $10^{3 \cdot 5}$ or more deaths.	40	55

It will be seen that even if Richardson's entries for wars with $10^{3 \pm 1/2}$ deaths are included: 1820—1884:109, 1885—1949:98, the general conclusion must be that Richardson's data show the later half of the observational period to be more warlike than the earlier half when measured by deaths. This must be so, since a single war of size 10^7 deaths can only be compensated for by 10,000 wars of size 10^3.

Sorokin's figures for 1826—1925 may be compared with those of Singer & Small for the same period. Sorokin's figures should be expected to be 3 to 4 times higher than Singer's and Small's because Sorokin included those wounded or missing. There is a rough approach to such a ratio in the data for 1901 to 1925. However the correlation between the two sets of figures is not at all perfect for the other three quarter centuries. Still a correlation of the logarithms of the numbers from the two sources produced a correlation coefficient of .94.

Singer's and Small's analysis covers the wars of Western and Westernized nations from 1816 to 1965, provided such wars were big enough. They demand at least 1000 military deaths to include a non-colonial war, and a nation is only considered participant in such a war if it experienced 100 or more battle-deaths or had 1000 or more soldiers in the field.

Concerning colonial (and imperial) wars they were only included if the colonial power had at least 1000 military deaths per year.

Singer's and Small's (1972) listing of battle-deaths further confirmed the trend of increasing war activity in the period 1816—1965. Although the total number of wars declined from the first to the second half of the period, the total war activity was higher in the second period both in terms of battle-deaths and in terms of nation months at war. Although this result is influenced by the growing number of nations included and their growing population, this factor does not explain the major part of the jump from 1.5 million battle deaths 1816—1890 to 28 millions 1891—1965.

In a more detailed breakdown the authors worked with five periods of 30 years' duration. During the first period 1816—1845 the battle deaths amounted to 245,000 for an average number of 27.1 nations. The two following figures were respectively more than three times bigger and more than twice as big. The fifth and final period covered the years 1936—1965 and had 18 million battle deaths for an average number of 80.4 nations (p. 191 Table 8.2).

If, as suggested by Boulding (1962), wars are less appropriate to an industrial civilization, then it must be said that so far this has not shown itself in less deadly wars or in less costly preparations for war.

There may, however, be an upper limit of tolerable violence. Klingberg (1966) used historical statistics for the period 1618 to 1918 in a study of losses of lives accumulated in loser nations at the end of a war. He found «some evidence» suggesting that modern nations surrender before they have lost 3—4% of their total population.

He noted, however, that some wars in the period investigated had resulted in much higher losses to the loser.

8.3 Population and Technology

The growth of the human population before the latest few centuries is only superficially known and can usually only be approximately estimated by taking into account the carrying capacity of the economy or similar assumed or observed population determinants. From about 1650 more specific estimates appear, and in general precision and validity may be assumed to increase with time. From estimates and facts concerning world populaton one important generalization seems well-founded:

From the origin of the species homo sapiens up to the middle of the twentieth century, although setbacks cannot be excluded, growth has tended to be exponential, with larger and larger absolute additions per unit of time.

From 1650 to 1750 world population is estimated to have increased about 34% per century to 728 millions. From 1750 to 1850 the increase is estimated at 61% per century. Finally from 1850 to 1950 world population is estimated to have grown from 1171 to 2486 or 112% per century. From 1950 to 1970 the growth of world population took place at the rate of 2% increase per year or 624% increase per century. If continued to 2050, this would give a world population more than seven times as large as the 1950 population.[3]

The increase in technology during modern times has tended to proceed at still higher annual rates. Consider as one illustration the development from 1820 to 1960 in the ability to kill at a distance (Table 8.4). In the course of 140 years this ability increased from 4 km in 1820 to 19,608 km in 1960, corresponding to more than 6% annual increase.

Table 8.4 Killing radius 1820—1960 in kilometers

1820	4
1840	6
1860	8
1880	11
1900	15
1920	539
1940	3251
1960	19,608

Estimated on basis of Hart in Allen (1957), assuming (cf. Svalastoga 1974, pp. 118—122) .0168 annual growth rate 1807—1910 and .094, from 1918 to 1960.

Andreski (1964) stressed the growth of the two factors as long enduring and influential trends in the history of mankind. He noted that the growth of knowledge in general depended on the development of larger nations providing larger areas of peace, and this again could in the past only be produced by wars of conquest.

Boulding (1964) emphasized the view that war represents a social mechanism adapted primarily to the agrarian period of human civilization. Boulding considered wars inappropiate both to the pre-agrarian and to the post-agrarian (industrial) civilization. Wars were seen as the tools whereby a small population of city dwellers could secure the surplus coming from a large agrarian populaton.

It is particularly hard to secure reliable evidence on pre-agrarian warfare. For this reason considerable variation exists in the views presented on the deadliness and the frequency of such warfare. Boulding seemingly assumes a pre-agrarian absence or near absence of major warfare.

Hobhouse, Wheeler & Ginsberg (1965, 1915) concluded in their classic empirical survey that war is «probably» not so common at the lowest as at the higher (agrarian) stages of civilization. But the few and small wars that took place may well have been accompanied by a higher percentage violent deaths at the hunting stage and at the lowest agrarian stages as compared to agrarian plow-using civilizations (ibid, pp. 228, 232).

Warner (1958, 1937) estimated the number of war deaths in an aboriginal Australian population at 200 over a 20-year period or an average of 10 war deaths per year in a total population of 3000 persons. Assuming a life expectation for this population of 25 years and consequently an annual death rate of $\frac{1}{25}$ or 4%, the total annual number of deaths becomes 120 persons. The war deaths thus constitute about 10% of all deaths, a rather high figure.

Wright (1965, 1942) took a definite stand on this issue: «it seems clear», he writes «that the collectors, lower hunters and lower agriculturalists are the least warlike[4] (p. 66)». He supported this statement by a study of 590 tribes (Cf. also ibid. p. 100).

Livingstone (1968) tended to underline the deadliness of pre-agrarian and early agrarian warfare. He cited several studies, but the evidence is hard to evaluate because of insufficient demographic information. The estimated war losses of 1% of the population per year or about 25% of all deaths for an American Indian tribe is a high rate of death due to war. So are likewise the reported figures from pre-conquest Mexico, with Cook as authority, of 15,000 annual war deaths in a 2 million population with a total annual number of deaths of 115,000.

Otterbein (1970) documented that political communities tend to increase their efficiency in warfare as they become more centralized. He showed that societies at the low end of a military efficiency scale rarely were expanding (only 3 out of 20 societies). Furthermore, these militarily less efficient societies in his sample were also less likely to register one-third or more of their warriers as battle deaths.

In Gouldner & Peterson's analysis of technology and ideology (1962) appears a set of correlations with a variable labeled «prevalence of war». From the correlations between 59 variables for 71 tribes investigated, the general trend of the data suggests that the less warlike tribes are also the less developed tribes. These are more often than not tribes where hunger was a real risk, where monogamy prevailed, and where fear of the dead prevailed, although all correlations in this set were modest, ranging only between − .1 and − .2. In contrast, the warlike tribes are more often tribes that keep slaves, have a chieftain institution, a codified set of laws, plutocracy, and agriculture. In this set correlations ranged from + .3 to + .5 (Cf. also Boalt & Herlin 1972, pp. 112—118).

Leavitt (1977) used data from the Human Relations Area Files, as Gouldner & Petersen also did. Leavitt studied 132 contemporary and historical societies.

Some support was found for the theory that frequency of external and internal war increases with increasing development of technology and increasing social differentiation.

If population, technology, and rate of social change are factors tending to increase the absolute and relative death toll of wars, then it should follow inversely that a small world population, a primitive technology, and a stagnant culture should produce not only absolutely but also relatively[5] fewer war deaths.

However, the effect of the factors mentioned may not be equally strong under all conditions. In particular, a small world population and a primitive technology are no protection against wars if the population is concentrated in hamlets within one day's walking distance or less from each other.

It follows that the factors population, technology, and rate of change can still be considered conducive to violence even if some or all pre-agrarian tribes can be found to have engaged in wars that killed off much larger parts of the population of warring nations or of its losers than has been documented for any modern large scale war.

There seems to be an emergent consensus on the importance of the two factors: population and technology to the amount of violence in territorial conflicts. The anthropologist Montagu, the sociologist van den Berghe, and the biologists Lorenz and Tinbergen all stressed the aggravating impact of these two factors (cf. sec. 1).

North (1970) emphasized the many strong and various effects that seems to be caused by population and technology. Population growth accompanied by technological advancement tends to contribute to rising demands, specialization, expansion of national interests, territorial competition, ideologies, arms races, and wars (p. 496). He furthermore stressed the importance of national differences in the rates of change of population and of technology and their social impact.

One reason for the dominant position given to population and technology may be that the power of a nation depends vitally on just these two factors.

In fact at a first approach it seems possible to write the equation for the power of a nation (cf. also Boulding 1962).

$$M = TP$$

where
$$M = \text{power}$$
$$T = \text{technology}$$
$$P = \text{population}$$

Since T carries the potential for a more rapid growth than P, it seems reasonable to attach greater weight to T than to P. This weighting may be further strengthened by considering the very real possibility that some part of the population may react negatively to the offensive or defensive actions of the nation (Boulding 1962):

$$M = T^a P^b$$

and $a > b$

But a nation is not equally strong at all points in space. It is usually strongest at its homebase and its strength declines with increasing distance from the homebase (cf. Stinchcombe on killing radius and Boulding (1962) on the Loss of Strength Gradient).

This circumstance explains why empirical research regularly reveals that proximity is associated with war risk. As Russett (1967) says, proximity is not a cause of war «but it makes nations salient to each other providing them with issues over which they can fight if other capabilities are low and with the opportunity to make their power felt on each others territory» (p. 201).

The strategic importance of superiority in population and technology was at least indirectly stressed by Clausewitz (1832—1834). Clausewitz devoted Book 3, Chapter 8, of his work to a very emphatic assertion on the importance of being superior to the enemy in numbers. «Sie (die Zahl) ist in der Taktik wie in der Strategie das algemeinste Princip des Sieges» . . . It is listed as the first law of strategy that as many troops as possible should be reserved for each battle.

In the fifth book (chapter four) there is a reference to the increased importance of infantry during the seventeenth century, owing to the improvement in firearms.

Vincent (1947) rejected the hypothesis that it is the function of wars to alleviate the pressure of a population on its resources. This hypothesis is rejected both because most wars of the past had losses that were replaced by natural increase over a few years and because most wars disturbed or destroyed the economic system, thereby diminishing the resources available.

8.4 Rate of Change

The dependence of the strength of a nation on technology and population implies that national strength is a changeable quantity. In particular, nations may change their technology and population at unequal rates and thereby become stronger or weaker than their neighbors; in both cases the balance of peaceful interaction may be disturbed (Svalastoga 1978).

The most emphatic statement of the thesis that differential rates of change in the form of «political lag» deserved attention as an outstanding cause of war comes from Quincy Wright. Wright noted a general tendency for political and legal adjustments to lag behind economic and cultural changes. The violent consequences of this lag could be observed in primitive and historic societies, but its importance had increased over time due to expansion of contacts (population growth?) and the technology-conditioned acceleration of change. The influence from Ogburn is notable. Actually Wright referred both to Ogburn's Social Change 1922, and to Ogburn's & Nimkoff's sociological textbook (Wright 1942, pp. 1284—1286). Galtung (1964) pointed to differences in growth rates among nations as the most likely cause of status inconsistency and hence according to his theory indirectly also a cause of war.

Wallace (1972) performed a correlation and dependence-analysis of a set of war-related factors in a sample of 28 nations. He concluded that the wide discrepancies in national growth rates in regard to population and economy have the effect of sharply intensifying violence. From his correlation tables it can be seen that this can be explained as a direct effect, and as an indirect effect through a measure of status inconsistency among nations.

Sorokin's theory of war and revolutions likewise put major emphasis on social change.

Sorokin's main theory, covering both wars and revolutions, is that both these variants of violence are «logical and factual consequences of the state of disintegration of the crystallized system of relationships» (1937, Vol. 3, p. 261).

The causes of such states of disintegration were seen as sets of combined factors. The Ideational-Sensate factor was not sufficient. But Sorokin contended that «the periods of transition from the Ideational to the Sensate or from the Sensate to the Ideational phase of culture are the periods of notable increase of war activities and war magnitude». His own study seemed to him to confirm this theory (Sorokin, 1937, pp. 374—6).

He inferred that the main insurance against wars is the «crystallization» of the system of cultural values and of social relationships (op. cit. p. 380). Crystallization of the system means (p. 18) that there is a definite system of rights and duties, functions (conduct), and social position for each member.

As an empirical generalization he noted in addition that there is a tendency towards more extreme war scores (more violence) for a nation when it is expanding and growing than when it is declining (P. 364).

Vayda (1968) presented a functional theory of war whereby war is seen as a response activated when certain essential variables in a social system threaten to leave or have already left their tolerable range of variation. War is functional to the extent the essential variables are restored to a tolerable range after the war. Such intolerable imbalances might well be more frequent in very small preliterate societies numbering rarely as much as 1000 persons than in modern macrosocieties and might also be simpler to redress during a war with a neighboring tribe. Several anthropologists have explained war among Bedouins as happening when disparities in camel ownership become intolerable and correspondingly for the Plains Indians when disparities in horse ownership became intolerable. In small groups demographic deviations threatening the survival of the group may well be the background for the many reports of wife-stealing expeditions.

130

8.5 Interaction

Wright's formal theory on the probability of war may perhaps best be described as an interaction theory. Wright elaborated an equation where the left side measured the probability of war between any two nations. This probability was presented as a function of altogether eight factors. Most of these factors were difficult to measure. They referred to the following characteristies:

1) War expectation (1 factor)
2) Mutual attraction (1 factor)
3) Similarity (4 factors)
4) Interaction (1 factor)
5) Ease of attack (1 factor)

Wright made an attempt to guess the values on each factor for a set of larger nations in July 1939. The result as given in Appendix 40 in his book is encouraging, but considerable measurement problems are still unsolved. It may be inferred from Wright's equation that war risk between two given nations is greater the more prevalent the expectation of war in each nation, and the more easily they can attack each other, but the factors of attraction, interaction, and similarity keep aggressive actions in check — if they are strong enough.

Timasheff (1965) also mentioned the importance of international interaction for the prevention of war (cf. sec. 7.1). In particular, he recommended migration as a remedy for the avoidance of wars arising from population pressure.

When nations interact, the interaction, may be more or less advantageous to each of the nations involved. In particular such interaction in terms of trade may create conflicts and these conflicts may at times lead to war. (Russett (1967) concluded his empirical investigation to the effect that trade *could* be a cause of war.

However, in inspecting his data in regard to major wars (5,000 deaths or more) he found no case of such wars among nations that were both strongly interdependent and strongly similar.

Wallensteen (1973) showed that the seven nations most often engaged in war 1920—1968 were also among the elite in participation in foreign trade. This does not contradict the general thesis here defended that mutually rewarding interaction builds a bulwark against war, because such interaction produces greater similarity and greater mutual attraction.

8.6 Territorial Cost

Robinson (1972) contended that the empires built by European powers were based on the philosophy that empires should be controlled cheaply or not at all.

European powers could control large areas of the world cheaply and with few troops because they could find influential cooperating groups in their colonies.

Without the voluntary or enforced cooperation of governing elites in the colonies, economic resources could not be transferred, strategic interests protected, or xenophobic reaction and traditional resistance to change contained.

Decolonization was explained in terms of the growing ability of the independence movement in the colonies to disrupt the arrangements for collaboration. In India and Africa up to 1947 there was, according to Robinson, an abundance of indigenous collaboration.

Around the middle of the twentieth century the prospective gains in territorial control began to decrease in value because of the increasing costs of such gains. Great powers found it much harder to defeat weaker states and, as suggested by Robinson, to find supporters among the conquered. In 1830 France conquered Algeria with 30,000 men. In 1962 no victory could be secured with 20 times as many men.

The causes seem to be (Huntington 1962, Knorr 1975):

1) Nuclear self-restraint of superpowers
2) Rivalry of superpowers
3) Diminished legitimacy of superpower use of force
4) Spread of nationalism

9. On Violence

> «No Man is an Iland, intire of it selfe; every man is a peece of the Continent, a part of the maine; if a Clod bee washed away by the Sea, Europe is the lesse, as well as if a Promontorie were, as well as if a Mannor of thy friends or of thine owne were; Any Mans death diminishes me, because I am involved in Mankinde; And therefore never send to know for whom the bell tolls; it tolls for thee».

> John Donne (Devotions 1624) Citation from Devotion 17. See Donne, J., Devotions Ed. A. Raspa, Montreal, 1975, University.

9.1 Review of Theories and Findings

In section 1 it was suggested that all attempts at explaining violent behavior in general could be classified according to the emphasis given to five major sets of variables or factors as causes or accelerators or amplifiers of violent behavior.

These five factors or variable sets were:

1) Organism
2) Environment
3) Population
4) Technology
5) Change

In section 2 the operational definition of violence to be used in this volume and introduced already in section 1 was put to use in an attempt to measure the demographic importance of death from the following five causes:

accidents, suicide, homicide, hierarchical violence, and territorial violence.

It was concluded that during the period 1900—1959 or 1901—1960 violent death thus defined constituted 7% of all deaths in United Kingdom, 10% of all deaths in France, 19% of all deaths in Germany, and 22% of all deaths in Russia (USSR). The more hypothetical character of the last figure was stressed.

Section 2 in addition noted the pioneering work of Lewis Fry Richardson, elaborated the defence of limiting the analysis to violent death, and went on to consider the importance of social factors in mortality generally. A subsection discussed various measures of the cost of violent deaths.

In section 3 attention was concentrated on operational violence and in the main centered on data stemming from the USA, England and Wales, France, and Sweden. Although each of the three varieties of operational violence, accidental death, suicide, and homicide, is treated separately in later sections, section 3 was needed in order to stress factors that were either hypothesized or documented to be related to deaths from operational violence in general.

The customs governing the activities of persons during transport, at home, at work, and during recreation help define tolerated mortality risks. With other customs, other risks and also fewer or more deaths occur from operational violence.

The deaths from operational violence are one part of the total cost of operating a social system.

If homo sapiens had been born with genes not so easily reconcilable with aggressive behavior as is now normal, then social systems could possibly operate at lower human costs. Whitlock (1971) considered that crimes of violence, suicide, and deaths by accidents were manifestations of the quality and quantity of aggression in a society. In particular road behavior was interpreted as in part determined by an aggressive drive leading to defence of territory, i.e. the driver's own car. This biological hypothesis is difficult to demonstrate. It has been simpler to demonstrate that those who die from accident, suicide, or homicide are more often than others not married, not middle class, not sober, and not of the female sex.

Among the deaths from operational violence the accidental deaths deserve special attention. It is probably an underestimate to assert that in the world as a whole 2 million people die each year from accidents.

The trend from about 1860 and up to about 1950 was found to be in the direction of a lower accident rate among the Western nations. A counter-tendency developed in Western Europe c. 1950—c. 1970. Around 1970 a shift to either steady state or decline was noticeable. It is the present author's expectation that Hair's hypothesis of a long-time decline will be confirmed.

The death toll from accidents are mainly found within one of four activity areas: transport, work, home, and recreation.

American accident statistics for the year 1956 showed that transport produced most accidental deaths (45,000), followed by home (26,000), work (14,000), and recreation (11,000).

Later statistics as tabulated by the World Health Organization or by national institutions rarely publish statistics that allow a distribution by major activities as above.

Compared to the amount of time spent on transport, the accident rate per person per hour or more simply the number of deaths per hour for population constant becomes higher than for the other three activity categories.

This is so because preferred modes of transportation are rather risky. Thus Sowby computed the riskiness of the private car in England c. 1960 as about 11 times higher than that of the railroad. Studies of seamen's accidents both in Norway and in Sweden documented that seamen who die from accidents most frequently die while leaving or returning to the ship or while ashore rather than on board the ship.

The high risk in road traffic is commonly ascribed to inappropriate speed, inadequate driver attention, traffic density, and failing visibility.

The risk of dying from accidents at home is particularly high for persons aged 65 years or older. The typical home accident with a fatal outcome is a fall.

A Danish study (Pedersen 1967) listing all accidents, lethal and non-lethal, by place of occurrence inside the home, reported the living-room as the place with the highest accident rate, but if frequency of use had been taken into account, it is possible that stairs would prove to be the most risky place in the home. In regard to work risk, large factories seem to be more accident-prone than small factories. Overtime work may be another negative factor. In contrast, factories that pay better than average or employ more females than average tend to have fewer accidents both in the USA, in India, in Japan, and in Hungary.

Some recreations may be highly hazardous. Thus according to Sowby's computations professional boxing would kill 70,000 persons out of 1000 million persons if each person were exposed to such boxing for one hour.

Lethal accidents hit mostly males, and the highest incidence is commonly between ages 0—5, 15—24, and at age 80 and higher.

Studies of suicide have documented that certain personal characteristics make suicide more likely: male sex, old age, divorced, single, or widowed, and childless. These are all characteristics that suggest a lower than average degree of integration in society if one assumes, as seems plausible, that the male sex is slightly less integrated in society than the female sex (compare the sex difference in crime). The disintegrating effect of disease was the most plausible explanation for a correlation disease-suicide appearing in Rudfeld's material (Rudfeld 1962, cf. World Health Organization Chronicle 1975, pp. 193—198). A study of Bombay gave support to the theory that fatalism is an effective antidote to suicide.

Suicide is an important cause of death. In particular, compared with the rate of homicide in Western Europe suicide is usually from 10 to 30 times more frequent. It is difficult to establish the presence or absence of a trend in suicide rate because of the tabus and other norms frequently surrounding it. The present author follows Hair in the assumption of a steady state with fluctuations. Thus, as is clearly shown in the English figures and frequently noted in the literature, the suicide rate declines in wartime and climbs up in times of economic depression. The English records of suicide for the twentieth century were shown to come rather close to a sinus curve.

Among social system characteristics the unsettling effects of war and economic depression were mentioned; researchers have also pointed to urbanism and the Protestant religion as positively related to suicide. Suicide is said to be contagious. Attempts at suicide not resulting in death are 7—8 times as frequent as suicides.

The two most important theories aiming to explain suicide were found to be the American ecological theory and the European sociological theory advanced by Durkheim. The ecological theory has the advantage that it can easily incorporate both characteristics of the social system and individual characteristics. At the same time Durkheim's (1897) theory still remains the best sociological explanation of suicide available.

In section 6 Homicide is assumed, chiefly on the basis of English data, to be negatively related to industrialism and urbanization and therefore considerably more rare now in Europe then was probably the case in earlier centuries. Homicide is now so rare in major European nations that its contribution to the total violence toll is almost negligable, accounting probably for only 2% of all deaths due to operational violence. Victims of homicide are more often males than females. The same is the case among the offenders. Those killed are most frequently the killer's relatives, friends or acquaintances. No specific homicide theory seems to exist. Theories used to explain homicide have been either general violence theories (frustration-aggression theory, subculture of violence theory, cf. sec. 1) or Durkheim's suicide theory, where the anomic situation has been assumed to be not only favorable to suicide, but also to homicide.

In sections 7 and 8 the topics dealt with are revolution and war, and an interesting problem is whether these two mass phenomena do possess common characteristics. Although most contributions in this field discuss either revolution or war but not both, it is still a legitimate question. In 1965 a positive response was already given by Timasheff, who contended that both for revolution and war the antecedents included serious conflict, rejection of peaceful means by at least one party, and the expectation of victory by both parties to the conflict. In Timasheff's opinion these characteristics made both revolution and war in principle controllable.

Both hierarchical and territorial violence expose or (hierarchical) seem to expose young males, and in particular young males of higher than average social status, to a higher level of risk than others.

Coming to Hierarchical violence in section 7, it is noted that such violence has tended to decline with increasing industrialization. Such increase has created stronger state organizations and also through democratic decision-making, avoided extreme conflicts, and provided numerous avenues for peaceful settlement of conflicts, and hence fewer revolutions and fewer deaths from hierarchical violence.

Sorokin's figures document that recent centuries do not usually show a maximum of hierarchical violence. Bank's series of successful coups d'état and revolutions 1815—1966 tell the same story of revolutions as rare events in the industrial world. Gurr documented the reduced death toll from civil strife among the highly developed nations as compared with those less developed. Students of revolutions have tended to focus on amount of social change while students of violence focus on the demographic cost.

When one approaches the problem of conditions favoring hierarchical violence, no factor seems to be more frequently mentioned than some form of inequality or heterogeneity.

Both Plato and Aristotle pointed to this factor as a cause of violent upheavals. Machiavelli warned princes against the special risks of subject populations characterized by extreme inequality of status. To Tocqueville inequality was the very fountain and fundamental cause of revolutionary activity.

Russett documented a correlation of about .5 between a Gini index of inequality and number of violent deaths per million.

A similar finding, this time with log population as associated predictor, was published by Sigelmann & Simpson.

On the whole the conclusion seems inescapable that inequality breeds violence, but also that three-quarters of the variation remains unexplained when inequality has been taken into account.

In particular, Marx (1850) had already stressed the braking effect of an economic boom regardless of state of inequality, and in Marx (1859, p. 9) one finds a rather explicit hypothesis on the differential rates of change between the «forces of production» and the «relations of production» as related to social violence.

Ellwood, Geiger, Sorokin, Olson, Chirot & Ragin, Davies, and Galtung stressed various aspects of social change as related to revolutionary activity.

Feierabend & Feierabend produced measures of rate of modernization and civic disorders and found a correlation of .65. Although direct tests or other documentations seem non-existent, it still seems reasonable to infer from the downward trend of hierarchical violence in the Western World and from the higher rates of violent disorders in developing countries that the increase in scientific understanding and technological capacity has produced political systems with higher survival rate than was typical of the Middle Ages in Europe and is still typical of many non-European areas.

Although no formal test has been performed, it seems that considerable inferential data suggest the conclusion that revolutionary activity or public disorders are contagious activities. They frequently spread far and fast in modern times helped by modern inventions, in particular, television.

An important factor in any public disorder is the size, material equipment, and morale of the defending or repressive forces. In a modern industrial society these three factors tend to make the defending forces vastly superior against violent apponents.

In section 8 dealing with territorial violence or war, the same problem is raised as for each of the four other causes of violent death: Is there a trend in the degree of violence due to war, i.e. in the rate of violent deaths due to war relative to the size of the population? It will be noted that we have described the most likely trend in both homicide and hierarchical violence as a declining trend, and that we found a long-term decline c. 1860 — c. 1950 for accidental deaths, a decline that may well continue after a brisk rise in the period 1950—1970, and even for suicides nothing more threatening than the continuation of a steady state was regarded as probable.

In estimating the war deaths (military and civilian) relative to population, a radically different long-term trend is documented by all sources here investigated. The main source is Sorokin, who himself for theoretical reasons (nothing can increase for ever) rejected the notion of one-directional trends and preferred curvilinear interpretations. However, as will be seen, his own data reveal convincingly a long-term increasing casualty rate from war. While Sorokin's estimate of casualties per year and per million inhabitants is at most 30 for France, England, Austria-Hungary, and Russia in the twelfth century, growing to at most 160 per year per million in the sixteenth century, all later centuries reveal higher figures, even the so-called peaceful nineteenth century (Table 8.1, cf. Table 8.2). The validity of this trend was considered supported by data collected independently by Wright, Richardson, and Singer & Small.

Was World War II the upper limit of the long-term trend? This question has not yet received an answer. Boulding's contention that wars are inappropriate to an industrial civilization still remains to be tested either by wars escalating into a total destruction of the species man, or by a gradual abstention from war in conflict resolutions in the interest of common survival.

Sorokin documented rather comprehensively the frequency, duration, and casualty rates characterizing the wars of a major part of the agrarian past of Europe.

It seems much more difficult to arrive at valid evaluations of the war activity of pre-agrarian societies. It is obvious that the pre-agrarians could not kill so many as were killed in agrarian or industrial period wars, but it is not so obvious that the number of deaths relative to population was lower at that time than later. In particular, if tribes lived close to each other the handicaps of primitive technology and small warrior population may not be large enough to prevent a total annihilation of one tribe by another. This possibility does not negate the influence of technology and population on territorial violence, but suggests certain limits to such influence. Even for fairly recent times the positive correlation of spatial closeness and teritorial violence is well documented.

Differential rate of change in population and technology produces international imbalance, because these factors are main determinants of national power. Both Sorokin and Wright emphasized social change as related to war. Wright inspired by Ogburn emphasized differential change rates, whereas Sorokin was more concerned with his general cyclical theory, in which the periods of transition were seen as violence-prone. In Wright's theory on the probability of war there appeared a set of factors that make for peace rather than war. They are clearly included from the more general consideration that the growth of mutual attraction between populations depends on mutually rewarding interaction. Such interaction likewise promotes similarity. Another possible peace factor is the increasing cost of space conquered.

Among the five causes of death by violence discussed here, two seem definitely to decline with increasing industrialization, viz. homicide and hierarchical violence, while one, suicide, may be preserving a steady rate of occurrence over long periods of time. The two most problematic violent causes of death are accidents and wars (territorial violence). accidents are problematic because they take such a large number of lives each year, and because accidents, although in principle controllable, are difficult to avoid with the set of risk-taking customs in existence. It should be remembered that the world average per year and million population is not likely to be below 500. With a world population of 4000 millions this indicates that at least 2 million lives are lost each year due to accidents, usually in principle avoidable. Each 10th year the accumulated world loss from accidents, is 20 million lives or about the same as the total battle deaths in England, France,

Germany, and Russia (USSR) 1900—1960 (cf Table 2.2).

Territorial violence or war is the only one of the causes of violent death for which we have been unable to discover any important trend other than the long-term one of an increasing number of deaths from war per capita and per year. Again, since wars are the work of men and since it is known that radical behavioral change is possible in man, war must be deemed in principle controllable. The difficulty is that the dominant values in the value hierarchy of the nations of the world seem to include many more strongly held values thatn that of war-avoidance.

This is the case because some wars to some nations will either seem to be or actually are a net gain. In other words som types of violence persist because they are highly rewarded.

It may be useful to take note of the rather impressive documented similarity between the three varieties of operational violence and of the less extensive, but still relevant, similarity between the two varieties of mass violence: hierarchical and territorial violence.

It was documented in sections 3—6 that the three major types of operational violence — accidental death, suicide, and homicide show rather far-reaching similarity in their empirical correlates and in the theoretical causation assumed or inferred. Sex is a factor in all of them, so is age, although the relation between age and type of death varied. A further common factor is what might be termed health, including reduced reactivity through alcoholism. More hypothetical is the assumption of a heightened level of aggression. Strictly empirical is the protective function of the married state. So is also the similar function of middle class status. The assertion of dependence of operational violence on risk customs is of course more theory than proven fact but a very plausible theory. Even the Durkheimian explanation of suicide in terms of the theoretical variables integration and control, seemingly applicable to homicide, could perhaps be applied to accidents too. Certainly if social integration and control may be said to be stronger or in a state closer to optimum integration in the middle class and in marriage than elsewhere, one could accept tentatively a Durkheimian interpretation of operational violence in general.

Mass violence, defined as deaths from hierarchical violence and from territorial violence, reveals a male proponderance in the Western World. There is also a correlation with age involved as for operational violence. Both in hierarchical and in territorial violence those who die in battle seem to have been close to 100% male in the Western World throughout its known history. Civilian losses may have been more evenly distributed between the sexes. A common relation to social status was also noted.

As the general theorists have suggested, we must assume a socially rewarded aggressiveness in the average human being. It will in hierarchical violence be influenced by the amount of internal inequality of a popualtion, but in the case of territorial violence by the degree of inequality between populations. Technology and rate of change are important to both of them. As the cost of conquest of territory seems to have increased, so similarly has the cost of obtaining hierarchical power by violence.

Apart from these common or similar causations some factors have been pointed to as relevant for war only (population size and population density). Hierarchical violence in the form of revolution, civil disorder, or terrorism may well be contagious and has been mentioned as such by theorists. In contrast, territorial violence was never referred to as contagious in the literature used for this study. Still both the historical reports on the Viking age and on the Victorian age seem to suggest that the taste for violent conquest might be stimulated not only by the expectation of gain but also by the education in the strategy and tactics of conquest given by victorious neighbors.

Archer & Gartner (1976) did establish a higher tendency to commit homicide after a war than before in combatant nations. The wars analyzed were World War I, World War II, and 11 minor wars. The theory that war breeds violence was strenghened.

9.2 The Explanation of Violence

In section 1 the consensual trend in violence theory was stressed. The present author fully accepts the importance of the five variable sets of consensual theory. Since much still depends on how the variables are further defined, and how they are related internally and to other variables, it seemed useful here to state dogmatically the present author's position. It is particularly influenced by van den Berghe and by Montagu, with William Fielding Ogburn as an always important source of inspiration.

In the interaction between the human organism and the social environment the human species, and more particularly its male part has developed customs of aggressive and risk-taking behavior tending to increase the toll of violent deaths.

Aggression and risk-taking may in addition have other, positively valued, functions. The more aggressive person may be more likely to advance science, art, and industry, to lead social movements or political parties, and to invent or propagate new beliefs.

The more risk-taking person may be more likely to save lives, to deliver goods on time, and to seek out new adventures.

The degree to which man's violence-related customs depend on his genetic constitution cannot yet be stated. None of the empirical studies of aggression cited above have been able to solve this problem.

The weight of the evidence seems, however, to suggest that the social causes of violence are the most important and increasingly more important causes.

The aggressive and risk-taking customs produce some violence (violent deaths) even in the absence of hierarchical or territorial imbalances. However, the general level of operational violence is further increased because of the reduction of operational efficiency introduced by alcohol customs, by disease, and by social disintegration.

The aggressive and risk-taking customs also produce a certain level of hierarchical and territorial violence. Increasing technological capacity produces more stable and more responsive governments. As a consequence, hierarchical violence has declined in the Western world. Territorial violence, in contrast, is strongly increased by population growth, by the growth of technology, and by the acceleration of change.

Over time the strong growth of population, with usable space resources growing more slowly, staying steady, or declining, increases competition for scarce resources both within and between nations. Simultanously man's increasing technological efficiency has made him a more dangerous animal, capable of setting forces in motion that may be hard to control. He has become at the same time both more constructive and more destructive in capacity. His culture has revealed a tendency towards an accelarated rate of change, in particular within the area of science and technology. Human adaptation to this change rate requires a higher level of social skills than that needed in slowly changing cultures. Maladaptation creates conditions favoring violence.

Furthermore, although all parts of industrial systems change and all social systems change, the rate of change may vary, and such differential speed, particularly in regard to technological innovation, produces violence between nations.

This happens because even a modest technological superiority can win wars and consequently be highly rewarded.

Territorial violence in the Western World has tended to increase over the centuries. Since the increase is produced by man, he possesses the capacity to control war. The motivation is inefficient and can only be developed by an increased level of cosmopolitan integration.

9.3 The Social Control of Violence

By control of violence will here be understood measures that make it possible to reduce the absolute and relative number of deaths due to accidents, suicide, homicide, hierarchical violence, and territorial violence.

It will be assumed that such control is to some extent already possible at the present time.

In regard to accidents, transportation by private car is the most risk-filled activity. Such accidents will be reduced up to 50% to the extent that drunken driving can be brought under control by legislation, education, and/or new inventions of sobering medicines.

Segregation of traffic according to speed is another life-saving technique (cf. Hvidtfeldt & Sterner 1974.)

The rather moderate tendency towards drunken driving in Norway compared to other Western countries has been explained as a consequence of the restrictive legislation whereby any driver discovered with more than the legal amount (.5g/l) of alcohol in the blood is imprisoned for at least three weeks (Christensen et al. 1978.)

The high risk of transport was dramatically shown in the Scandinavian reports on seamen. It seems likely that an impoved round-the-clock harbor dock welfare service for foreign seamen could materially increase the survival chances of seamen. In industrial work the further introduction of protective instruments that are both safe and easy to use while working might likewise save lives, so might further legislation and education in favor of safety. In the home the shockingly high number of falls resulting in death should be of interest to architects and construction engineers with a view to the gradual introduction of safer constructions, e.g. fewer stairs.

In sport and entertainment safety may frequently be a low priority value. These activities can probably only be made safer by legislation and education. According to Thygerson (1977) two-thirds of American drowning victims do not know how to swim.

Thygerson is probably one of the most up-to-date and elaborate sources in general on the prevention of conventional accidents and on the reduction of hazards due to natural disasters.

Suicide depends in part on the social environment and in part on the individual concerned. Suicide should therefore be partly controllable to the extent that it is possible to create social environments characterized by a high level of integration. Since such social reconstruction is time-consuming, a simpler way may be to provide special protective environments for persons who are suffering from nervous or other handicapping diseases or who are highly dependent on alcohol or drugs.

Homicide can probably be brought further down in some parts of the

Western World to the extent that the total number of handguns carried around can be reduced.

The successful reduction of hierarchical violence may have come about in part because of the greater horizontal and vertical mobility of industrial societies as compared to agrarian societies. Further safety valves exist in the party system democracies. When parties are distributed from right to left, the chance is small that important social maladjustments go unnoticed.

To control war a higher level of interaction among the nations of the world seems a minimum requirement. A mutually rewarding interaction would perhaps not be the fastest way of producing a world government, but it is probably the only way of producing a government of the world that will last.

In the meantime war activity can be in part controlled to the extent that the power elite among nations can reach and maintain a certain level of cooperation.

An important principle in accident prevention and perhaps in all attempts to prevent violent death is the application of Pareto's «law» originally applied by Pareto to the measurement of the distribution on income and wealth (Pearson 1969, cf. Svalastoga 1965). Pareto's law includes the assumption that a small part of the population accounts for a large part of the total income or wealth. Pearson documented that industrial accidents reveal the same general tendency: a few main causes tend to account for a large part of the accident expenses. He cited one study which showed that only 2% of the number of injuries accounted for 50% of the cost, and one-third of the injuries accounted for 94% of the total cost. It is therefore of prime importance to isolate the vital few causes and not waste time on near-zero correlates, or on causes with only modest effects.

10. References by Section

SECTION 1

Ardrey, R. *The territoral imperative,* New York 1966 (orig. ed. 1960).

Aristotle. *Politics.* Loeb. ed.

Asher, L. Chemistry of violence, *Psychology today,* vol 12, no 6, p 46, 1978.

Baer, D. The sociobiology debate. *Science* 1978, 200, p 382.

Ball-Rokeach, S. J. Values and violence, *American sociological review* 1973, 38:736 – 49.

Bandura, A. *Aggression. A social learning analysis.* Englewood Cliffs, N J 1973.

Berkowitz, L. *Aggression: a social psychological analysis.* New York 1962.

Björl, E. Den ökonomiske imperialismeteori. *National-ökonomisk tidsskrift,* 1970, 108: 35 – 45.

Boulding, K. E. *The meaning of the twentieth century. The great transition.* New York 1964.

Boulding, K. E. *The impact of the social sciences.* New Brunswick, N J 1966.

Boulding, K. E. Am I a man or a mouse – or both? Montagu, M F A, *Man and Aggression,* London 1968, pp 83 – 90.

Brzezinsky, Z. Nye tendenser i storpolitikken. *Fremtiden,* 1976, 31: 4 – 10.

Calhoun, J. B. Population density and social pathology, *Scientific American,* 1962, 206:139 – 148.

Carstairs, G M. Overcrowding and human aggression. Graham & Gurr (eds.) *Violence in America,* 1969, pp 593 – 602.

Choucri, N. & North, R C *National growth and international violence,* London 1975.

Christie, N. *Hvor tett et samfunn,* 1.2, Oslo 1975.

Corning, P A & Corning, C H. Toward a general theory of violent aggression. *Social science information,* 1972, 11:7 – 33.

Council of Europe. *Violence in society.* Tenth Conference of Directors of Criminological research institutes, Strasbourg, 1972. Strasbourg 1973.

Crook, J H. The nature and function of territorial aggression. Montagu M F A (ed.) *Man and aggression,* London 1968, pp 141 – 178.

Danielsen, E. *Vold – en ond arv?* Copenhagen 1978.

Darwin, C. *The origin of species by means of natural selection,* London 1929 (1859).

Davies, J C. Aggression, violence, revolution, and war. Knutson, J. N. (ed.) *Handbook of political psychology,* San Francisco 1973, pp 234 – 260.

Derriennic, J – P. Theory and ideologies of violence. *Journal of peace research,* 1972, 9: 361 – 374.

Deutsch, K W. Power and communication in international society. Reuck, A. & Knight, J. (eds.) *Conflict in society,* London 1966, pp 300 – 316.

Dollard, J., et al. *Frustration and aggression,* New Haven 1961 (1939).

Ehrenkranz, J., Bliss, E. & Sheard, M. Plasma testosterone: Correlation with aggressive behavior and social dominance in man. *Psychosomatic medicine,* 1974, 36: 469 – 475.

Ehrlich, P R. & Ehrlich, A H. *Population, resources, and environment,* San Francisco 1970.

Eisenberg, L. Psychiatric intervention. *Scientific American,* 1973, 229, 3: 116 – 127.

Elliş, L. The decline and fall of sociology, 1975 – 2000. *American sociologist*, 1977, 12: 56 – 66.

Erlanger, H. (a) The empirical status of the subculture of violence thesis. *Social problems*, 1974, 22: 280 – 292.

Erlanger, H. (b) Social class and punishment. *American sociological review*, 1974, 39: 68 – 85.

Feierabend, I K. & Feierabend, R. *Cross national data bank*, New York 1965.

Feierabend, I K. ed. *Anger, violence and politics*, Englewood Cliffs 1972.

Feierabend, I K., Feierabend, R L. & Nesvold, B A. Social change and political violence. Cross natinal patterns. Graham, H D. & Gurr, T R. (eds.) *The history of violence in America*, New York 1969, chapter 18, pp 632 – 687.

Freud, S. *Jenseits des Lustprincips*, 1940 (1917). Ges. Werke 13.

Freud, S. *A general introduction to psychoanalysis*. New York 1953 (1920).

Galtung, J. A structural theory of aggression. *Journal of peace research*, 1964, 1: 95 – 119.

Galtung, J. *A structural theory of revolution*, Rotterdam 1974.

Gastil, R D. Homicide and a regional culture of violence. *American sociological review*, 1971, 36: 412 – 427.

Goode, W J. The place of force in human society. *American sociological review*, 1972, 37: 507 – 519.

Graham, H D. & Gurr, T R. (eds.) *Violence in America*, Washington DC 1969.

Graham, H D. & Gurr, T R. Conclusion. Graham & Gurr (eds.) *Violence in America*, 1969 pp 621 – 644.

Grofman, B N & Müller, E N. The strange case of relative gratification and potential for political violence. *American political science review*, 1973, 67: 514 – 539.

Gunn, J. *Violence in human society*, Devon 1973.

Hackney, S. Southern violence. Graham & Gurr (eds.) *Violence in America*, 1969, pp 387 – 404.

Haddon, W., Suchman, E A. & Klein, D. *Accident research methods and approaches*, New York 1964.

Hawkins, G. & Ward, P. Armed and disarmed police: Police firearms policy and levels of violence. *Journal of research in crime and delinquency*, 1970, 7. 188 – 197.

Hawley, A. Cumulative change in theory and in history. *American sociological review*, 1978, 43: 787 – 796.

Heshka, S. & Nelson, Y. Interpersonal speaking distance. *Sociometry*, 1972, 35: 491 – 498.

Kornhauser, W. *The politics of mass society*, Glencoe Ill. 1959.

Kreutz, L. & Rose, R. Assessment of aggressive behavior. *Psychosomatic medicine*, 1972, 34, no 4.

Kuznets, S. Population, income, and capital. *International social science bulletin*, 1954, 6 (2): 165 – 170.

Loftin, C. & Hill, R H. Regional subculture and homicide. An examination of the Gastil-Hackney thesis. *American sociological review*, 1974, 39: 714 – 724.

Lorenz, K. *Das sogenannte Böse*, Wien 1973 (1963).

McCarthy, J D., Galle, O R. & Zimmern, W. Population density, social structure, and interpersonal violence. *American behavioral scientist*, 1975, 18: 771 – 791.

Maccoby, E. & Jacklin, C. *The psychology of sex differences*, Stanford, California 1974.

McDougall, W. *An introduction to social psychology*, 12th ed. London 1917 (1908).

Magura, S. Is there a subculture of violence. *American sociological review*, 1975, 40: 831 – 836.

Malthus, T R. *Population: The first essay* (1798), Ann Arbor, Michigan 1959.

Marx, K. *Zur Kritik d. politischen Oekonomie*, Berlin 1859.

Mayhew, B H. & Levinger, R L. Size and density of interaction in human aggregates. *American Journal of sociology*, 1976, 82: 86 – 110.

Mickiewicz, E. *Handbook of Soviet social science data*. New York 1973.

Miller, W B., Geertz, H. & Cutter, H. Aggression in a boys' street corner group. *Psychiatry*, 1961, 24:4: 283 – 298.

Montagu, M F A. *The nature of human aggression*, New York 1976.

Murray, D R. Handguns. *Social problems*, 1975, 23: 81 – 92.

Myers, K., Hale, C S., Mykytowycz, R & Hughes, R L. The effects of varying density . . . and space on sociality and health in animals. In ESSER, *Behavior and environment*, New York 1971.

National Commision on the causes and prevention of violence. Final report, Washington 1969.

Newton, G D. & Zimring, F E. *Firearms and violence in American life*, Washington DC (1969).

Nieburg, H L. Uses of violence. *Journal of conflict resolution*, 1963, 7: pp 43 – 54.

Ogburn, W F. *Social change*, Gloucester, Mass. 1964 (1922).

Parsons, T. Certain primary sources and patterns of aggression in the social structure of the Western world. *Psychiatry*, 1947, 10: 167 – 181.

Persky, H., Smith, K. & Basu, G. Relation of psychological measures of aggression and hostility to testosterone production in man. *Psychosomatic medicine*, 1971, 33: 265 – 277.

Petersen, W. *Population*. New York 1961.

Russell, C. & Russel, W M S. *Violence, monkeys, and man*, London 1968.

Schilling, W R. Technology: Technology and international relations. *Encyclopedia of the social sciences*, 1968, 16: 589 – 598.

Scott, J P. *Aggression*. 2nd ed. Chicago 1975.

Seitz, S. Firearms, homicides, and gun control effectiveness. *Law & Society review*, 1972, 6: 595 – 613.

Selg, H. (ed.) *The making of human aggression*, transl. London 1975 (1971).

Shah. S. & Roth, L. Biological and psychophysiological factors in criminality. Glaser, D. (ed.) *Handbook of criminality*, pp 101 – 174. Chicago 1974.

Simmel, G. Conflict. Transl. by K. Wolf. *The web of group affiliations*. Transl. by R. Bendix, Glencoe Ill., 1955 (1908).

Smith, J M. The evolution of behavior. *Scientific* American, 1978, 239: 136 – 145.

Smith, P K. & Connolly, K J. Social and aggressive behaviour in preschool children as function of crowding. *Social science information*, 1977, 16 (5): 601 – 620.

Sorokin, P A. (ed.) *Explorations in altruistic love and behavior*, Boston 1950.

Steinmetz, S. & Straus, M. The family as cradle of violence. *Society*, 1973, 10: 50 – 56.

Storr, A. *Human destructiveness*, London 1972.

Svalastoga, K. Differential rates of change and violence, France and Germany 1820 – 1920. *Acta sociologica*, 1978, 21: 23 – 33.

Thomle, E. *Hver syvende dansker*. Jyllandsposten 30/4-1979. (Study conducted by Observa and supervised by Preben Wolf.)

Tiger, L. & Fox, R. *The imperial animal*, London 1972.

Tilly, C. Collective violence. Graham & Gurr (eds.) *Violence in America*, 1969, pp 5 – 34.

Timasheff, N S. *War and revolution*, New York 1965.

Tinbergen, N. On war and peace in animals and man. *Science*, 1968. 160:1411 – 1418.

Toby, J. Violence and the masculine ideal. *Annals, Amer. Acad. Pol. soc. Sc.*, 364, 1966.

Van den Berghe, P L. Bringing beasts back in: Towards a biosocial theory of aggression. *American sociological review*, 1974, 39: 777 – 788.

Van den Berghe, P L. (a). Comments. *American sociological review*, 1975, 40: 674 – 682.

Van den Berghe, P L. (b) *Man in society* New York 1975.

Van den Berghe, P L. Territorial behavior in a natural human group. Social science information, 1977, 16 (3/4): 419 – 430.

Vandenberg, S G. Hereditary factors in normal personality traits (as measured by inventories). *Recent advances in biological psychiatry*, 1967, 9: 65 – 104.

Washburn, S L. *Ape into man*, Boston 1974.

Weiss, B. *Food and mood. Psychology today*, 1974, 8, no 7, p 60.

Welch, S. & Booth, A. Crowding as a factor in political aggression. *Social science information*, 1974, 13 (4/5): 151 – 162.

Wilson, E O. *Sociobiology*, Cambridge, Mass. 1975.

Winslow, R. W. *Society in transition*, New York 1970.

Wolf, P. *Vold i Danmark og Finland 1970/71*, Copenhagen 1972. (Mimeographed).

Wolf, P. *On individual victims . . . four Scandinavian countries 1970 – 1974*, Copenhagen 1976.

147

(Mimeographed).

Wolfgang, M E. *Patterns of criminal homicide,* Philadelphia 1958.

Wolfgang, M E. & Ferracuti, F. *The subculture of violence. Towards an integrated theory in cirminology,* London 1967.

Wolfgang, M E. (ed.) Patterns of violence. *Annals of the American Academy of political and social science,* 1966, no 364.

Ziming, F. Is gun control likely to reduce violent killings? *University of Chicago law review,* 1968, 35: 721 – 737.

SECTION 2

Biraben, J N. Essai sur l'évolution démographique de l'URSS. *Population,* 1958, 13, numero 2 bis, pp 29 – 62.

Bouthoul, G. *Traité de polémologie,* Paris 1970.

Chagnon, N. Yanomamö social organization and warfare. Fried, M. (ed.) *War,* New York 1968, pp 109 – 159.

Dublin, L. & Lotka, A. *The money value of a man,* New York 1930.

Eason, W W. The Soviet population today. An analysis of the first results of the 1959 census. *Foreign Affairs,* 1959, 37 (4): 598 – 606.

Erdmann, K D. Die Zeit der Welt-kriege, Gerhardt (ed.) *Handbuch der Weltgeschicte,* vol 4, Suttgart 1976.

Historical statistics of the United States. *Colonial times to 1970.* Washington DC 1975.

Hollingsworth, T H. A demographic study of the British ducal families. *Population studies,* 1957, 9: 4 – 26. (A summary is to be found in Glass, D. & Eversley, D. (eds.) *Population in history* London 1965).

Hollingsworth, T H. The demography of the British peerage. *Population studies,* 1964 – 5, 18, no 2, Supplement, pp 1 – 108.

Livingstone, F B. The effects of warfare. Fried, M. et al. (eds.) *War,* New York 1968.

Lorimer, F. *The population of the Soviet union.* League of Nations, Princeton 1946.

Menninger, K. *Man against himself,* New York 1966 (1938).

Mickiewicz, E P. *Handbook of Soviet social science data,* New York 1973.

Petersen, W. *Population,* New York 1961.

Pressat, R. Surmortalité biologique et surmortalité sociale. *Revue francaise de sociologie,* 1973, 15 no. spec., 103 – 110.

Reynolds, D J. The cost of social accidents. *Journal of the Royal Statistical society,* Series A, vol 4, no 119, 1956, pp 393 – 408.

Richardson, L F. *Statistics of deadly quarrels,* Pittsburgh 1960.

Sauvy, A. *Théorie générale de la population,* 1,2, Paris 1956.

Urlanis, B. *Wars and population.* Transl. Moscow 1971.

Vallin, J. *La mortalité par génération en France, depuis 1899. (Travaux et documents, cahier no 63).* Paris 1973.

SECTION 3

Boalt, g. & von Euler, R. *Alkoholproblem,* Stockholm 1959.

Chesnais, J C. *Les morts violentes en France depuis 1826,* Paris 1976. (Institut national d'études démographiques. Travaux et documents, Cahier 75.)

Danmarks statistik. *Statistiske undersøgelser, nr.37. Dødelighed og erhverv.* (Mortality and occupation) Copenhagen 1979.

Fekjær, H O. *Ny viten om alkohol,* Oslo 1980.

Finnish foundation for alcohol studies and world health organization, Europe. *International statistics on alcoholic beverages. Production, trade, and consumption 1950 – 1972,* (Helsinki 1977).

Geckler, S., et al. *Fordeling av levekårene. Socialforskningsinstituttet.* Publikation 82, bind 2, Copenhagen 1978.

Geertinger, P. & Voigt, J. Dødsfald i badekar. *Nordisk kriminalteknisk tidsskrift,* 1969, 39: 21 – 31.

Goldberg, L. Alkohol och trafikrisker. *Statens offentliga untredningar,* 1970: 61, Stockholm 1970.

Haberman, P. & Baden, M. Alcoholism and violent death. *Quarterly journal of studies on alcohol,* 1974, 35, 1, Part A: 221 – 231.

Hackney, S. Southern violence. Graham & Gurr (eds.) *Violence in America,* 1969, ch. 14, pp 387 – 404.

Haddon, W. et al. *Accident research,* New York 1964.

Hair, P. Deaths from violence in Britain. A tentative secular survey. *Population studies,* 1971, 25: 5 – 24.

Historisk statistik för Sverige. *Statistiska översiktstabeller,* Stockholm 1960.

Humphrey, J A. & Kupferer, H J. Pockets of violence − exploration of homicide and suicide. *Diseases of the nervous system,* 1977, 38: 833 – 837.

Iskrant, A. & Joliet, P. *Accidents & homicide,* Cambridge, Mass. 1968.

Jacobziner, H. Childhood accidents and their prevention. *AMA Journal of diseases of children,* 1957, 93: 647 – 665.

Johansson, S. *Den vuxna befolkningens kostvanor,* Stockholm 1970.

Laurell, H. Effects of small doses of alcohol on driver performance. *Accident analysis and prevention,* 1977, 9: 191 – 201.

Lederman, S. *Alcool, alcoolisme, alcoolisation. Paris 1956 – 1964.* Institut national d'études demographiques. (Travaux et documents, Cahier 29, 41.)

Lint, J. & Schmidt, W. Alcoholism and mortality. Kissin, B. & Begleiter, H. (eds.) *The biology of alcoholism,* vol 3, New York 1971 – 1977, pp 275 – 305.

Lærum, H., Sørensen, T. & Rasmussen S. Selvmord i Danmark. En analyse . . . selvmord 1972. (With summary in English). *Ugeskrift for læger,* 1980, 142: 37 – 41.

National center for health statistics, Series 20, no 8a, Rockville, Md. 1970.

Norman, L G. *Road traffic accidents,* Geneva 1962.

Office of population censuses and surveys. Occupational mortality. The registrar general's supplement for England and Wales 1970 – 72. Series DS, no 1, London 1978.

Peller, S. Birth and death among Europe's ruling families since 1500. Glass, D V. & Eversley, D E C. (eds.) *Population in history,* London, 1965, pp 87 – 100.

Pernanen, K. Alcohol and crimes of violence. Kissin, B. & Begleiter, H. (eds.) *The biology of alcoholism,* vol 3, New York 1971 – 1977, pp 351 – 444.

Porterfield, A L. Traffic fatalities, suicide, and homicide. *American sociological review,* 1960, 25: 897 – 901.

Reigstad, A., Bredesen, J. & Lunde, P. *Ulykker, alkohol og nervemedisin,* Oslo 1977.

Sowby, F D. Radiation and other risks. *Health* physics, 1965, 11: 879 – 887.

Starr, C. Social benefit versus technological risk. *Science,* 1969, 165: 1232 – 1238.

Straus, R. Alcoholism and problemdrinking. Merton, R K. & Nisbet, R. (eds.) *Contemporary social problems,* 4th ed. New York 1976, pp 181 – 217.

World Health Organization. *International classification of diseases. Manual* (8th reviison, 1965), 1, 2. Geneva 1969, 1967.

Zylman, R. A critical evaluation of the literature on «Alcohol involvement» in highway deaths. *Accidents analysis & prevention,* 1974, 6: 163 – 204.

SECTION 4

Ammundsen, E. & Jespersen, I. Ulykker i hjemmene i København. *Nordisk hygienisk tidsskrift, 1953, 250 – 260.*

Arner, O. Dødsulykker blant sjømenn, Oslo 1970.

Backett, E M. *Les accidents domestique, Geneve 1967.* (Organisation mondiale de la santé: Cahiers de santé public, no. 26.)

Bull, J P. Accidents and their prevention. Hobson, W. (ed.) *The theory and practise of public health*, 4th ed., London 1975, pp 367 – 375.

Bø, O. *Road casualities*, Oslo 1972.

Ceder, A. & Livneh, M. Further evaluation of the relationship between road accidents and average daily traffic. *Accident analysis & prevention*, 1978, 10: 95 – 109.

Chesnais, J C. & Vallin, J. Evolution récente de la morbidité dues aux accidents de la route (1968 – 1977). *Population*, 1977, 32: 1239 – 1265.

Dalgaard, J B. Kulite dødsfald ved selvmord, ulykker, og drab. Copenhagen 1961. *Acta Jutlandica* 33: 3, Medical Series 11.

Dreyer, K. & Nørregaard, S. A. Deaths by accident among children in Denmark 1931 – 1955. *Danish medical bulletin*, 1957, 4: 219 – 230.

Enig, R. Ulykkesfugle og accident-proneness (A – P faktoren). *Ugeskrift for Læger*, 1954, 116: 607 – 613.

Iversen, L. *Arbejdsulykker i Danmark 1960 – 1972*, Copenhagen 1974.

Jensenius, H. Statistiske undersøgelser af ulykkestilfælde. *Bibliotek for Læger*, 1957, 149: 1 – 87.

Koshal, R K. & Koshal, M. A note on Hungarian industrial accident experience. *Accident analysis & prevention*, 1974, 6: 93 – 94.

Lossing, E. & Goyette, R. Review of 1000 home accidents. *Canadian journal of public health*, 1957, 48: 131 – 140.

Organization for Economic Cooperation and Development (OECD). Road research. New research on the role of alcohol and drugs in road accidents. By an OECD Road research group. Chairman: G A. Smith. Paris 1978.

Otterland, A. A sosiomedical study of the mortality in merchant seafarers. Göteborg 1960. *(Acta medica scandinavica*, vol 167, suppl.357).

Pedersen, E. Flere hjemmeulykker? Foredrag Oslo 21. febr. 1967. *Socialt arbeid*, 1967, 41: 188 – 196.

Roberts, H J. *The causes, ecology, and prevention of traffic accidents*, Springfield 1971.

Rumpf, H, Rempp, H. & Wiesinger, M. *Technologische Entwicklung*. Vol 1 – 3. Göttingen 1976, (Kommission für Wirtschaftlichen und Sozialen Wandel).

Shaw, L. & Sichel, H S. *Accident proneness*, Oxford 1971.

Svenson, O. Risks of road transportation in a psychological perspective. *Accident analysis & prevention*, 1978, 10: 267 – 280.

Svalastoga, K. Differential rates of growth and road accidents. *Acta sociologica*, 1970, 13: 73 – 95.

Thygerson, A L. *Accidents and disasters, causes and countermeasures*, Englewood Cliffs, New Jersey 1977.

Vallin, J. & Chesnais, J C. Les accidents de la route en France. Mortalité et morbidité depuis 1953. *Population*, 1975, 30: 443 – 478.

Waller, J. A. Falls among the elderly. *Accidents analysis & prevention*, 1978, 10: 21 – 33.

Whitlock, F A. *Death on the road. A study in social violence*, London 1971.

SECTION 5

Allen, R C D. *Mathematical economics*, 2nd ed. London 1959.

Barrett, G V. & Franke, R H. «Psychogenic» death. *Science*, 1970, 167: 304 – 306.

Baechler, J. *Les suicides*, Paris 1975.

Cavan, R S. *Suicide*, Chicago 1928.

Douglas, J D. *The social meanings of suicide*, Princeton N J 1967.

Dublin, L I. *Suicide*, New York 1963.

Durkheim, E. *Le suicide*, Paris 1897.

Faris, R E L. *Social disorganization*, 2nd ed. New York 1955.

Ferri, E. *L'omicidio – suicidio*, 4th ed. Torino 1895.

Halbwachs, M. *Les causes du suicide*, Paris 1930.

Hartelius, H. Suicides in Sweden 1925 – 1950. *Acta psych. & neur. Scand.*, 1957, 32: 151 – 181.
Henry, A F. & Short, J F. *Suicide and homicide. Some economic, sociological and psychological aspects of aggression*, New York 1954.
Iga, M. et al. Suicide in Japan. *Social science & medicine*, 1978, 12A: 507 – 516.
Kato, M. Selfdestruction in Japan. *Folia psych. et neur. Japonica.* 1969, 23: 291 – 307.
Kayser, C J. *Om selvmord*, Copenhagen 1846.
Kruijt, C S. The suicide rate in the Western world since world war II. *The Netherland's journal of sociology*, 1977, 13: 55 – 64.
Lalli, M. & Turner, S H. Suicide and homicide. A comparative analysis by race and occupational levels. *Journal of criminal law criminology, & police science*, 1968, 59: 191 – 200.
Morselli, E. (Discussion participation, meeting of 22 November 1885.) Actes 1. Congrés international d'anthropologie criminelle. Torino 1886 – 87, pp 202 – 208.
Morselli, E. Suicide. An essay on comparative moral statistics. (Abridged transl. of Italian orginal ed.) New York 1975, 1882.
Ogburn, W. & Thomas, D. The influence of the business cycle on certain social conditions. *Journal, American statistical association*, 1922, 18: 324 – 340.
Pai, D N. Epidemiology of suicide, homicide, and accidents. *Indian journal of medical science, 1967, 21: 117 – 122.*
Pærregaard, G. *Selvmordsforsøg og selvmord i København*, 1, 2. Copenhagen 1963.
Retterstøl, N. *Selvmord*, Oslo 1970.
Rudfeld, K. Suicides in Denmark 1956. *Acta sociologica*, 1962, 6: 203 – 214.
Schmid, C F. *Suicides in Seattle, 1914 to 1925. An ecological and behavioristic study*, Seattle 1928.
Schmid, C F. & Van Arsdol, M D. Completed and attempted suicides. A comparative analysis *American sociological review*, 1955, 20: 273 – 283.
Stengel, E. *Suicide and attempted suicide*, London 1965.
Verkko, V. Henki-ja pahoinpitelyrikollisuuden . . . 1. Suomi ja naap, Helsinki 1931.
Verkko, V. *Verbrechen wider das Leben und Körperverletzungsverbrechen. 1. Finnland u. die benachbarten Länder*, Helsinki 1937. (Abbreviated transl. from Finnish origial ed.)
Verkko, V. *Homicides and suicides in Finland and their dependence on national character*, Copenhagen 1951.

SECTION 6

Archer, D. & Gartner, R. Violent times and violent acts. *American sociological review*, 1976, 41: 937 – 963.
Bohannan, P. (ed.) *African homicide and suicide*, Princeton, N J 1960.
Bruun, K. *Alkohol i Norden*, Stockholm 1973.
Chesnais, J C. L'homicide dans le monde. *Revue francaise des affairs sociales*, 1975, 117 – 140.
Hanawalt, B A. Violent death in fourteenth- and early fifteenth-century England. *Comparative studies in society and history*, 1976, 18: 297 – 320.
Hansen, J P. Hart. *Drab i Danmark 1946 – 1970*, Copenhagen 1977.
Palmer, S. *A study of murder*, New York 1960.
Siciliano, S. *L'omicidio*, Padova 1965.
Svalastoga, K. Homicide and social contact. *American journal of sociology*, 1956, 62: 37 – 41.
Svalastoga, K. *Prestige, class, and mobility*, Copenhagen 1959.
Wolfgang, M E. *Patterns in criminal homicide*, New York 1966 (1958).
Wolfgang, M. Homicide. *International encyclopedia of the social sciences*, 1968, 3: 490 – 495.

SECTION 7

Baechler, J. *Les phénoménes revolutionnaires*, Paris 1970, (Le Sociologue, 19.)
Banks, A S. *Cross-polity timeseries data*, Cambridge, Mass 1971.
Brinton, C. *The anatomy of revolution*, New York 1952 (1938).

Brown, R M. The American vigilante tradition. Graham & Gurr (eds.) *Violence in America,* 1969 vol 1, pp 121 – 169.

Chirot, D. & Ragin, C. The market, tradition, and peasant rebellion: The case of Romania in 1907. *American sociological review,* 1975, 40: 428 – 444.

Cohan, A S. *Theories of revolution,* London 1975.

Dahrendorf, R. Über einige Probleme d. soziologischen Theorie d. Revolution. *European journal of sociology,* 1961, 2: 153 – 162.

Davies, J C. Toward a theory of revolution. *American sociological review,* 1962, 27: 5 – 19.

Davies, J C. The J-curve of rising and declining satisfactions . . . Graham, H D. & Gurr, T R. (eds.) *Violence in America,* Washington DC 1969, pp 547-576.

Davies, J C. The J-curve and power struggle theories of collective violence. *American sociological review,* 1974, 39: 607 – 610.

Dumas, S. & Vedel-Petersen, K. *Losses of life caused by war,* Oxford 1923.

Edwards, L P. *The natural history of revolutions,* Chicago 1970 (1927).

Ellwood, A C. A psychological theory of revolutions. American journal of sociology, 1905, 11: 49 – 59.

Feierabend, I K. & Feierabend, R L. Aggressive behaviors 1948 – 1962. Journal of *conflict* resolution, 1966, 10: 249 – 271.

Galtung, J. A. *Structural theory of revolutions,* Rotterdam, 1974.

Geiger, T. *Die Masse und ihre Aktion,* Stuttgart 1926.

Good, W J. Mobilität u. Revolution. *Kölner Z. Soziologie,* 1966, 18: 227 – 252.

Gurr, T R. A comparative study of civil strife. Graham, H D. & Gurr, T R (eds.) *Violence in America,* 1969, vol 2, pp 443 – 486.

Gurr, R. & McClelland, M. Political performance. A twelve-nation study Beverly Hills 1971. *Comparative politics*series, vol 2, no 18.

Hibbs, D A. Jr. *Mass political violence. A cross-national causal analysis,* New York 1973.

Huntington, S P. Patterns of violence in world politics. Huntington, S P. (ed.) *Changing patterns of military politics,* Glencoe, Ill, 1962, pp 17 – 50.

Johnson, C A. *Revolution and the social system,* Stanford 1964.

Kirkham, J F., Levy, S G. & Crotty, W J. *Assassination and political violence.* Staff reports, National commission on the causes and prevention of violence, Washington D C 1969.

Klingberg, F L. Predicting the termination of war: Battle casualities and population losses. *Journal of conflict resolution,* 1966, 10: 129 – 171.

Laqueure, W. Revolution. *International encyclopedia of the social sciences*, 2nd ed., vol 13, New York 1968, pp 501 – 507.

Levy, S G. A 150 years study of political violence in the United States. Graham & Gurr (eds.) *Violence in America,* 1969, vol 1, pp 65 – 77.

Lodhi, A. & Tilly, C. Urbanization, crime, and collective violence in the 19th century France. *American journal of sociology,* 1973, 79: 296 – 318.

Marx, K. *Die Klassenkämpfe in Frankreich 1848 bis 1850.* Marx-Engels Werke, Bd 7, pp 9 – 107, Berlin 1973, 1850.

Marx, K. *Zur Kritik der politischen Oekonomie,* Berlin 1859. Marx-Engels Werke, Bd. 13, pp 3 – 160. Berlin 1974, 1859.

Marx, K. & Engels, F. *Manifest der Kommunistischen* Partei. Marx-Engels Werke, Bd. 4, pp 459 – 493, Berlin 1974, 1848.

Olson, M. Jr. Rapid growth as a destabilizing force, pp 215 – 227. Davies, J C. (ed.) *When men revolt and why,* New York 1971.

Pareto, V. *Mind and society,* New York 1963 (1916).

Pitcher, B, Hamblin, R. & Miller, J. The diffusion of collective violence. *American sociological review,* 1978, 43: 23 – 35.

Plato. *The republic.* Transl. H D P. Lee, London 1959.

Russett, B M. Inequality and instability. Davies, J D. (ed.) *When men revolt and why,* New York 1971.

Short, J. & Wolfgang, M. (eds.) *Collective violence, Chicago 1972.*

Sigelman, L. & Simpson, M. *A crossnational test of the linkage between economic inequality and political violence. Journal of conflict resolution, 1977,* 21: 105 – 128.

Synder, D. & Tilly, C. Hardship and collective violence in France 1830 to 1960. *American sociological review,* 1972, 37: 520 – 532.

Sorokin, P. *Die Soziologie der Revolution,* München 1928.

Sorokin, P. *Social and cultural dynamics, vol 3: Fluctuations of social relationships, war, and revolution,* New York 1962 (1937).

Spilerman, S. Structural characteristics of cities and the severity of racial disorder. *American sociological* review, 1976, 41: 771 – 793.

Stohl, M. War and domestic political violence USa 1890 – 1970. *Journal of conflict resolution,* 1975, 29: 379 – 416.

Tanter, R. & Midlarsky, M. A theory of revolution. *Journal of conflict resolution,* 1967, 11: 262 – 280.

Taylor, C L. & Hudson, M C. *World handbook of political and social indicators,* 2nd ed. New Haven 1972.

Tilly, C. Collective violence. Graham & Gurr (eds.) *Violence in America,* 1969, vol 1, pp 5 – 34.

Tilly, C. Revolutions and collective violence. Greenstein, F. & Polsbo, N. (eds.) *Handbook of political science,* vol 3, pp 483 – 555, Reading, Mass. 1975.

Tocqueville, A. de. *De la démocratie en Amerique* 1, 2, Paris 1951 (1835), (Ouvres 1.1, 1.2.)

Tocqueville, A. de. *Democracy in America,* (ed.) P. Bradley, 1.2. New York 1961.

Vierkandt, A. Zur Theorie der Revolution. *Schmollers Jahrbuch für Gesetzgebung,* 1922, 46:2: 19 – 41.

Zipf, G K. Wage distribution and the problem of labor harmony, Sorokin, P. (ed.) *Explorations,* Boston 1950, pp 333 – 346.

SECTION 8

Andreski, S. *Elements of comparative sociology,* London 1964.

Boalt, G. & Herlin, H. *Krigets Sociologi,* Stockholm 1972.

Boulding, K. *Conflict and defence,* New York 1962.

Boulding, K. *The meaning of the twentieth century,* New York 1964.

Clarke, R. *The science of war and peace,* London 1971.

Clausewitz, C. v. *Vom Kriege,* Berlin 1853 (1832 – 34).

Gouldner, A W. & Peterson, R A. *Notes on technology and the moral order,* New York 1962.

Hobhouse, L. T., Wheeler, G C. & Ginsberg, M. *The material culture and social institutions of the simpler peoples,* London 1965 (1915).

Knorr, K. *The power of nations,* New York 1975.

Leavitt, G. The frequency of warfare. *Sociological inquiry,* 1977, 47: 49 – 58.

Livingstone, F. B. The effects of warfare on the biology of the human species, Fried, M. et al. (eds.). *War, The anthropology of armed confliet,* N.Y. 1968 pp 3 – 15.

Munroe, T. A critique of theories of imperialism. Boulding, K E., *Essays in honor of K E B,* ed. M. Pfaff, Amsterdam 1976, pp 143 – 157.

North, C R. Wright on war. *Journal of conflict resolution,* 1970, 14: 487 – 498.

Otterbein, K F. *The Evolution of war,* New York 1970.

Robinson, R. Non-European foundations of European imperialism, Owen, E R J. & Sutcliffe, R B. (eds.) *Studies in the theory of imperialism,* London 1972, pp 117 – 140.

Russett, B M. *International regions and the international system,* Chicago 1967.

Singer, D. & Small, M. *The wages of war,* New York 1972.

Sorokin, P. *Contemporary sociological theories,* New York 1928.

Svalastoga, K. *The social system,* Copenhagen 1974.

Vayda, A P. Hypotheses about functions of war, Fried, M. et al. (eds.) *War, The anthropology of armed conflict,* New York 1968, pp 85 – 91.

Vincent, P. Guerre et population. *Population,* 1947, 2: 9 – 30.

Wallace, M D. Status, formal organization, and arms levels as factors leading to the onset of war

1820 – 1964. Russett, B M. (ed.), *Peace, war, and numbers,* London 1972.
Wallensteen, P. *Structure and war. On international relations 1920 – 1968,* Stockholm 1973.
Warner, W L. *A black civilization.* Rev. ed. New York 1958 (1937).
Wright, Q. *A study of war,* Chicago 1965 (1942).

SECTION 9
Christensen, P., Fosser, S. & Glad, A. *Drunken driving in Norway,* Oslo 1978. (Mimeographed.)
Hvidtfeldt, H. & Sterner, J. *Trafikuheld og trafikmiljø i boligområder,* Copenhagen 1974. (Rådet for trafiksikkerhedsforskning og Statens byggeforskningsinstitut.)
Pearson, M W. Pareto's law and modern injury control. *Journal of safety research,* 1969, 1: 55 – 57.
Svalastoga, K. *Social differentiation,* New York 1965.

Notes

SECTION 1

[1] Which in operational terms seems to have the same referent as «violence».

[2] $H = \dfrac{r_m - r_d}{1 - r_d}$

r_m = correlation among monozygotic twins
r_d = correlation among dizygotic twins

[3] Virginia, West Virginia, Kentucky, Tennessee, North Carolina, South Carolina, Georgia, Alabama, Mississippi, Louisiana, Arkansas.

[4] New England and most upper North states.

[5] Reprinted by permission.

[6] If individuals or groups or nations are ranked on two factors as either topdog (T) or underdog (U), these are the types possible.

[7] Reprinted by permission

SECTION 2

[1] Including suicide by murderer or execution of murderer as well as cases of multiple murder. Richardson did not include suicides.

[2] Pressat's expression about upper class advantage of 5—10 years is translated into 7.5 years' advantage, so that upper class life expectation is 32.5 years, and loower class life expectation is 25 years.

[3] Snakebites, Tiger attack.

[4] According to Chagnon most likely to be malaria.

[5] Except that *Annuaire* 1961 was used for 1947 values.

[6] On the basis of similar French observations.

[7] And also according to Urlanis (1971, p. 284, cf. p. 132). Urlanis, however, estimated non-military deaths at 10 million persons.

[8] Assuming 4.5 million deaths for the three years 1957, 1958 and 1959 not covered by Biraben.

SECTION 3

[1] r = Pearsonian rho

[2] In contrast a measure of alcoholism used in the American study correlated negatively $r = -.55$ with road accidental deaths.

[3] A 1968 report to the American Congress is cited. It documents that out of 2176 drivers in lethal single-accidents, i.e. not multiple accidents, stemming from four studies altogether, 67,5% had consumed alcohol, the majority even with more than 1.5 g/l alcohol concentration in the blood.

[4] Assumed to be caused by alcoholism and inadequate diet.

[5] According to Straus (1976), such decline was not noticed in the USA, where a steady state of 7.61. (2 gallons) pure alcohol per capita per year was maintained 1850—1960.

SECTION 4

[1] I am indebted to my distinguished colleague J. C. Chesnais for this observation.

[2] Reprinted by permission.

[3] For corrected mortality figures taking into account «mortalité tardive» crediting the year 1972 with 18,360 traffic deaths, an all-time annual maximum not yet (latest year of observation: 1976) beaten cf. Vallin & Chesnais (1975) and Chesnais & Vallin (1977).

[4] On this factor cf. Norman (1962, pp. 57, 58), who reported that excessive speed was recorded in 31% of all fatal accidents in the USA in 1959.

[5] Reprinted by permission.

[6] Including: Railway and vehicle

Railway and vehicle	66
Fall-drowning	199
Fall-injury	93
Accident to shop	211
Other accidents	82
Homicide or suicide or accident	63
	714

[7] Defined as «grave alcoholic abuse».

SECTION 5

[1] Variations over space are still more problematic because nations, even in the industrial part of the world, use different procedures in the registration of suicide and also in the registration of homicide and accident (World Health Organization, Chronicle 1975, 29:188—193). Several countries, including the United Kingdom and Norway, have no provision on the death certificate for recording suicide or homicide or accident.

[2] An urban social system is held to be more suicidal than a rural social system, because the urban system experiences a larger number of social contacts per unit of time (Halbwachs 1930, p. 509).

SECTION 6

[1] Oxford rolls 1296—1393 include 12 complete years.

SECTION 7

[1] PV = Population × Violence after having rescored each variable as mentioned above.

[2] $(100 \times 46 \times 100)^{1/3} = 77.19$

[3] Calculated using population estimates for midyears:

Year	Population (millions)	Deaths/Populatin $\times 10^6$
1833	14	1.9
1863	34	10.9
1893	67	6.6
1923	112	1.6
1953	160	.6

[4] Twenty-two European nations, 8 on or close to the American continent, 4 Asiatic, and 3 others.

[5] Countries of Eastern and Western Europe (except Spain and Portugal) plus USA, the English settled states of the British Commonwealth, and Israel.

[6] In this paragraph Pareto is quite certain about the general cause of revolutionary behavior. It

is said to be «sufferings» in the «subject class». However, Pareto then considers the possibilities: the more suffering, the more revolutionary activity or the more suffering the less revolutionary behavior, and he is not willing to accept any of them.

SECTION 8

[1] Sorokin defined casualties in war as number of killed and wounded, he did not include missing persons (1937, pp. 282, 307, 338, and 553).

[2] Edward III had only about 10,000 men at the battle of Crécy (1346), at Poiters (1356) his son (Edward, the Black Prince) had less than 6,000 warriors, and Henry V was victorious at Agincourt (1415) with 5,000 men (cf. Vincent 1947).

[3] The data used was already tabulated in Svalastoga (1974, Table 4,2 p. 109)

[4] Reprinted by permission

[5] Relative to population or to the total number of deaths.

Abstract

On Deadly Violence reports on theories and research on violence in general and on each of the five main types of violence: accidental death, suicide, homicide, hierarchical violence (revolution and repression), and territorial violence (war). Attention is limited to violence causing deaths. A search for trends and determinants of violence in general and its specific forms is made. War is the most threatening form of violence because its death-toll has been increasing for a long time. Accidental death is the most costly in terms of lives lost per year.

MAY 0 1907